Awakening the Remnant

Jonathan Mukwiri

TEACH Services, Inc.
www.TEACHServices.com

**PRINTED IN
THE UNITED STATES OF AMERICA**

World rights reserved. This book or any portion thereof may not be copied or reproduced in any form or manner whatever, except as provided by law, without the written permission of the publisher, except by a reviewer who may quote brief passages in a review.

Copyright © 2010 Jonathan Mukwiri
Cover Copyright © 2010 TEACH Services, Inc.
ISBN-13: 978-1-57258-636-9
Library of Congress Control Number: 2010932815

Published by
TEACH Services, Inc.
www.TEACHServices.com

Contents

Preface v

Error and Truth at War in the Church 1

Amusements and Secular Dressing 18

Worshiping Like Other Churches 50

Diet Reform is Not an Option 73

Urged to Worship on Sunday 96

Victory Over Sin Before Sealing 112

Obedience and Salvation Inseparable 136

Please prayerfully read this book and these memory verses

"Let us hear the conclusion of the whole matter: Fear God, and keep his commandments: for this is the whole duty of man" (Eccl. 12:13).

"Whether therefore ye eat, or drink, or whatsoever ye do, do all to the glory of God" (1 Cor. 10:31).

"Behold, I come quickly: hold that fast which thou hast, that no man take thy crown" (Rev. 3:11).

Preface

Awakening the Remnant is a book for Seventh-day Adventist saints as a last wake-up call before the close of probation. We are living in the most perilous times in the history of God's saints. It is out of much affliction and anguish of heart that I have written to you with many tears. It is not that by this awakening you should be grieved but that you might know the love of God who sends messengers. The contents of this end-time book may attract harsh treatment from some quarters of our church. The subjects addressed herein may be considered by some to be forbidden. While some will be awakened, others may denounce this book. Some may label the counsel herein as "judgmental" or "legalistic" or of "extreme views." These uncomplimentary labels have led many church leaders to remain silent while members remain in a deep sleep.

We have long remained in neutral positions about these subjects, but the saints need to be awakened lest we all perish. While unwritten and unspoken policies may prevent many serving theologians from addressing these subjects, it is left to us who are not in employed ministry to write on these subjects. Even for laymen, the likely attack from esteemed scholars in our church who may disagree should never be underestimated. It is clear though that a work of *awakening the remnant* must be done quickly.

Our Lord Jesus Christ has impressed me with the burden of *awakening the remnant*. When the Lord called me to write, "I was no prophet, neither was I a prophet's son" (Amos 7:14). I was not a pastor but a servant of Jesus Christ to all and especially to fellow Seventh-day Adventists. "Now the things which I write unto you, behold, before God, I lie not" (Gal. 1:20). Prayerfully read this book with your eyes upon Jesus.

"Time is short, and what you do must be done quickly. Resolve to redeem the time. Seek not your own pleasure. Rouse yourself! Take hold of the work with a new purpose of heart. The Lord will open the way before you. Make every possible effort to work in Christ's lines, in meekness and lowliness, relying upon Him for strength. Understand the work the Lord gives you to do, and, trusting in God, you will be enabled to go on from strength to strength, from grace to grace. You will be enabled to work diligently, perseveringly, for your people while the day lasts; for the night cometh in which no man shall work" (Ellen G. White, *Testimonies for the Church*, vol. 9, p. 200).

"What astonishing deception and fearful blindness had, like a dark cloud, covered Israel! This blindness and apostasy had not closed about them suddenly; it had come upon them gradually as they had not heeded the word of reproof and warning which the Lord had sent to them because of their pride and their sins. And now, in this fearful crisis, in the presence of the idolatrous priests and the apostate king, they remained neutral. If God abhors one sin above another, of which His people are guilty, it is doing nothing in case of an emergency. Indifference and neutrality in a religious crisis is regarded of God as a grievous crime and equal to the very worst type of hostility against God" (Ellen G. White, *Testimonies for the Church*, vol. 3, p. 280).

"I know that which I now speak will bring me into conflict. This I do not covet, for the conflict has seemed to be continuous of late years; but I do not mean to live a coward or die a coward, leaving my work undone. I must follow in my Master's footsteps" (Ellen G. White, *The Southern Work*, p. 10).

Jonathan Mukwiri
England, United Kingdom
September 2009

Chapter 1

Error and Truth at War in the Church

The great controversy that began in heaven has always been and remains on the question of worship. As members of the Seventh-day Adventist Church, we may deny open devil worship, but Satan knows that as long as we mix doctrines of error and truth while claiming to worship God, Satan will still be worshiped indirectly.

Error and truth are at war. Even the question of what constitutes the Word of God, from a remnant perspective, raises issues of error versus truth. Error advocates that Scripture excludes the writings of Ellen G. White as an authoritative source. As a result of this error, there is a growing objection to Ellen White's writings in the Seventh-day Adventist Church. To them that are captured by such error or not led by the Spirit of God, a reproof referring to say, "tea and coffee drinking is a sin" (*Counsels on Diet and Foods*, p. 425), is met with a fierce call of "show me where it says so in the Bible."

Scripture foretells an end-time gift of prophecy (Rev. 12:17, 19:10; Joel 2:28-32). Thus the writings of Ellen White are included in the overall source of scriptures for the remnant church. These writings of Ellen White are known in the remnant church as Testimonies or the Spirit of Prophecy. Before you make hasty objections about Ellen

Awakening the Remnant

White's writings being part of Scripture and, in the process, risk grieving the Holy Spirit that inspired all prophets, let us expound upon this.

Because the gift of prophecy is an identifying mark of God's end-time remnant church (Rev. 12:17) and because we believe that this gift was manifested in the ministry of Ellen White, as a Seventh-day Adventist Church, we are justified in referring to her writings as the Spirit of Prophecy or the Testimonies, even as we would to all inspired messages from God. To this end, therefore, one of our fundamental beliefs notes: "As the Lord's messenger, her writings are a continuing and authoritative source of truth which provide for the church comfort, guidance, instruction, and correction. They also make clear that the Bible is the standard by which all teaching and experience must be tested (Joel 2:28, 29; Acts 2:14-21; Heb. 1:1-3; Rev. 12:17, 19:10)."

In Bible times some prophets wrote books, which became part of the Bible. These biblical prophets include such notables as Moses, Jeremiah, Isaiah, Paul, and John. Others, however, such as Enoch, Elijah, and Elisha, wrote no books of the Bible, yet their messages and ministries are preserved in it. Still, there were prophets like the four daughters of Philip (Acts 21:9) whose messages have not been preserved in the Bible. And finally, there were prophets who actually wrote books that have not been preserved. They include Nathan and Gad (1 Chron. 29:29), Shemaiah (2 Chron. 12:15), Jasher (Joshua 10:13; 2 Sam. 1:18), Iddo (2 Chron. 9:29, 12:15), Ahijah (2 Chron. 9:29), and Jehu (2 Chron. 20:34).

But whether included in the Bible or not, the messages delivered by all categories of prophets were authoritative, inspired by the Holy Spirit with messages from God. Ellen White was also a true prophet. Though her writings are not a part of the Bible, yet like the non-biblical prophets above, her messages are nonetheless authoritative and form the broader category of scriptures.

Error and Truth at War in the Church

Moreover, in biblical language, all inspired writings, books of the Old Testament or the epistles that were by then being written to churches, were referred to as Scripture. Luke referred to the now Old Testament as scriptures: "And beginning at Moses and all the prophets, he expounded unto them in all the scriptures the things concerning himself" (Luke 24:27).

Peter referred to Paul's epistles as scriptures even though these by then were not yet formed into the Bible as we know it today: "And account that the longsuffering of our Lord is salvation; even as our beloved brother Paul also according to the wisdom given unto him hath written unto you; As also in all his epistles, speaking in them of these things; in which are some things hard to be understood, which they that are unlearned and unstable wrest, as they do also the other scriptures, unto their own destruction" (2 Peter 3:15, 16).

Ellen White's writings are not part of the Bible because they are simply not compiled into the Bible. However, to confine scriptures to only what we now call the Bible and exclude the inspired writings of Ellen White from the term scriptures would not be in keeping with biblical language used by the apostle Peter.

If you still find it hard to accept the Testimonies as God's scriptures, you are in danger of equating them to the devil's work. To the doubters, Ellen White wrote: "God is either teaching His church, reproving their wrongs, and strengthening their faith, or He is not. This work is of God, or it is not. God does nothing in partnership with Satan. My work . . . bears the stamp of God, or the stamp of the enemy. There is no halfway work in the matter. The Testimonies are of the Spirit of God, or of the devil. God Speaks Through Testimonies – We must follow the directions given through the Spirit of prophecy. We must love and obey the truth for this time. This will save us from accepting strong delusions. God has spoken to us through His Word. He has spoken to us through the Testimonies to the church, and through

Awakening the Remnant

the books that have helped to make plain our present duty and the position that we should now occupy" (*Evangelism*, p. 260).

Without the Holy Spirit, error and truth are impossible to distinguish. "The track of truth lies close beside the track of error, and both tracks may seem to be one to minds which are not worked by the Holy Spirit, and which, therefore, are not quick to discern the difference between truth and error" (Ellen G. White, *Selected Messages*, bk. 1, p. 202).

When studying the Word of God, we must always remember the following: "But the natural man receiveth not the things of the Spirit of God: for they are foolishness unto him: neither can he know them, because they are spiritually discerned" (1 Cor. 2:14). As Seventh-day Adventists, we have the truth, yet if error and truth are mixed together within us, it has to be explained by lack of the Holy Spirit working in us. We risk becoming mere scholars and intellectuals of the truth without really living the truth.

In view of this closeness of error and truth, the Spirit of Prophecy explains the fearful possibility of a so-called reformation that would plunge the church further into error. Ellen White wrote, "The enemy of souls has sought to bring in the supposition that a great reformation was to take place among Seventh-day Adventists, and that this reformation would consist in giving up the doctrines which stand as the pillars of our faith, and engaging in a process of reorganization. Were this reformation to take place, what would result? The principles of truth that God in His wisdom has given to the remnant church, would be discarded. Our religion would be changed. The fundamental principles that have sustained the work for the last fifty years would be accounted as error. A new organization would be established. Books of a new order would be written. A system of intellectual philosophy would be introduced. The founders of this system would go into the cities, and do a wonderful work. The Sabbath of course, would

Error and Truth at War in the Church

be lightly regarded, as also the God who created it. Nothing would be allowed to stand in the way of the new movement. The leaders would teach that virtue is better than vice, but God being removed, they would place their dependence on human power, which, without God, is worthless" (*Selected Messages*, bk. 1, p. 204).

Some in our church quarters do not see this fearful so-called reformation as the problem facing our church. Error argues that legalism is the biggest problem the church faces. Error makes the case that there is too much focus on doctrine, lifestyle standards, a fundamentalist approach to the Bible and Spirit of Prophecy, pillars of our faith, old-fashioned gospel, and victorious living.

Coming to the aid of error is the liberal left, often operating from within the church leadership. They seek to interpret our historical doctrines that stand as the pillars of our faith to align them with modern or new theology. This stresses love, acceptance, and inclusiveness. This destroys church unity by introducing a counterfeit unity that allows for error and truth to coexist.

Truth humbly claims that worldliness and a lack of conversion is the biggest problem facing the church. Truth makes the case that the problem is manifested in a failure to accept a plain "thus saith the Lord," a lowering of lifestyle standards, a patterning after the surrounding churches, a making of no effect the Spirit of Prophecy, rationalization of God's Word, and a loss of identity as a remnant church.

Coming to the aid of truth is the independent right, often operating without the church leadership. They seek to adhere strictly to our historical doctrines. This stresses law as the character of God, perfectionism through abiding in Christ, and uniqueness within the context of the remnant church. Often, out of desperation, this indirectly leads to the faithful members to separate from certain congregations to maintain purity. Teaching truth with zeal while counteracting error, often leads to ministers censoring members for what ministers

Awakening the Remnant

label "extreme views." Censor may lead to taking counsel: "Fearing that the faith of the believers would be endangered by continued association with these opposers of the truth, Paul separated from them and gathered the disciples into a distinct body, continuing his public instructions in the school of Tyrannus, a teacher of some note" (Ellen G. White, *The Acts of the Apostles*, p. 285).

We have gradually lost the adversarial relationship with the world that once distinguished us as a holy peculiar people, and we now embrace error instead of truth. Quench not the Spirit of God that speaks in this book. The inspired word tells us: "In every generation God has sent His servants to rebuke sin, both in the world and in the church. But the people desire smooth things spoken to them, and the pure, unvarnished truth is not acceptable. Many reformers, in entering upon their work, determined to exercise great prudence in attacking the sins of the church and the nation. They hoped, by the example of a pure Christian life, to lead the people back to the doctrines of the Bible. But the Spirit of God came upon them as it came upon Elijah, moving him to rebuke the sins of a wicked king and an apostate people; they could not refrain from preaching the plain utterances of the Bible,—doctrines which they had been reluctant to present. They were impelled to zealously declare the truth, and the danger which threatened souls. The words which the Lord gave them they uttered, fearless of consequences, and the people were compelled to hear the warning" (Ellen G. White, *The Great Controversy*, p. 606).

Those leaders who only understand doctrines or truth as interpreted by higher clergy or scholars from their conferences, and who lead members who only accept doctrines or truth as explained by ministers, find no need to study the Word of God to find out for themselves what the truth is. These take no lessons from the Bereans in Acts 17:10-11 who studied the Word to see if these things were so. If these dare make any study, only the church manual is their source of reference.

Error and Truth at War in the Church

The church manual that may be used as a guide has turned the creed to replace the Bible and the Spirit of Prophecy. Others who find it a controversy to study, prefer to let error and truth coexist. What then is the implication of error and truth existing among us? There are ten possible implications on either side; let us outline these for our future study.

First, we outline the possible implications of error:
1. Importance of obedience is downplayed.
2. Importance of character perfection is minimized.
3. Importance of distinctive Seventh-day Adventist doctrines is reduced.
4. Importance of lifestyle standards is lightly regarded.
5. Call to come out of Babylon is muted.
6. Message and mission of the church suffer.
7. The identity of God's special remnant church is imperilled.
8. God is robbed of His glory.
9. Sin and suffering are prolonged.
10. The Second Coming is delayed.

Second, we outline the possible implications of truth. Again, these are mentioned here for our future study and detailed understanding of these implications:
1. End time call to obey all of God's commandments by faith is promoted.
2. Character perfection brings glory to God.
3. Distinctive doctrines form a unified whole.
4. Lifestyle standards protect God's people from greater dangers.
5. Final call to separate from Babylon's false systems is made loud.
6. Message and mission of church are strengthened.
7. Identity of church is enhanced.

Awakening the Remnant

8. God is glorified by His people being in harmony with His message and with each other.
9. Sin and suffering is curtailed and shortened.
10. The Second Coming is hastened.

For everything we partake of as the remnants, we must intentionally, now more than ever before, subject it to the scrutiny of the Word of God. Those who cannot stand in truth now, when the Sunday law is passed, if not already, will apostate and give up their faith altogether. Is it possible to know now whether you will apostate then? Yes, you can know now, for we are clearly told that:

"Those who have yielded step by step to worldly demands and conformed to worldly customs will then yield to the powers that be, rather than subject themselves to derision, insult, threatened imprisonment, and death. At that time the gold will be separated from the dross. True godliness will be clearly distinguished from the appearance and tinsel of it. Many a star that we have admired for its brilliance will then go out in darkness. Those who have assumed the ornaments of the sanctuary, but are not clothed with Christ's righteousness, will then appear in the shame of their own nakedness" (Ellen G. White, *Prophets and Kings*, p. 188).

The question you may ask is, Are you willing to apply this inspired revelation to your own life and experience? Have we, as individuals or as a church, developed a tolerance for error, and have we as a result adjusted certain aspects in order to be less peculiar? Are we conforming to world demands step by step?

A closer examination of the problem reveals that the problem is how to address the problem. Most members who get a glimpse of the errors are deceived into believing that addressing the errors will cause disunity in the church. To these, unity is the absence of conflict. Such members dare not rise against questionable church policies lest they

Error and Truth at War in the Church

are seen as divisive or troublesome or anti-unity. The default position is to try and unite truth and error, and often remaining silent for the sake of unity.

If we try to unite error and truth, it can never be true unity; it will be a counterfeit unity. Paul warned against this in 2 Corinthians 6:14: "What fellowship hath righteousness with unrighteousness? and what communion hath light with darkness." Ellen White was emphatic on this matter: "Light and darkness cannot harmonize. Between truth and error there is an irrepressible conflict. To uphold and defend the one is to attack and overthrow the other" (*The Great Controversy*, p. 126). Certain church policies may not be questionable until subjected to Scriptures scrutiny. Like the Bereans (Acts 17:10, 11), we should subject all church policies to Scripture to avoid the danger of following tradition of men and worshiping God in vain (Mark 7:7).

Our identity is rapidly being eroded. The prophet said: "Seventh-day Adventists have been chosen by God as a peculiar people, separate from the world. By the great cleaver of truth He has cut them out from the quarry of the world, and brought them into connection with Himself. He has made them His representatives, and has called them to be ambassadors for Him in the last work of salvation. The greatest wealth of truth ever entrusted to mortals, the most solemn and fearful warnings ever sent by God to man, have been committed to them to be given to the world" (*Counsels to Writers and Editors*, p. 178).

If we are given this great truth to warn the world, by calling the other sheep into the flock, by calling them out of Babylon, what business do we have in embracing the errors taught in Babylon? Have some of us reached a level that we have so lost our identity that we see no errors? Take time to read these verses from the Word of God as you prepare to read the rest of this book:

Awakening the Remnant

"My people are destroyed for lack of knowledge: because thou hast rejected knowledge, I will also reject thee" (Hosea 4:6).

"And with all deceivableness of unrighteousness in them that perish; because they received not the love of the truth, that they might be saved" (2 Thess. 2:10).

"Man shall not live by bread alone, but by every word that proceedeth out of the mouth of God" (Matt. 4:4).

"If ye continue in my word, then are ye my disciples indeed" (John 8:31).

"But though we, or an angel from heaven, preach any other gospel unto you than that which we have preached unto you, let him be accursed" (Gal. 1:8).

"God hath from the beginning chosen you to salvation through sanctification of the Spirit and belief of the truth" (2 Thess. 2:13).

"As I besought thee to abide still at Ephesus, when I went into Macedonia, that thou mightest charge some that they teach no other doctrine" (1 Tim. 1:3).

"In all things shewing thyself a pattern of good works: in doctrine shewing uncorruptness, gravity, sincerity" (Titus 2:7).

"Go ye therefore, and teach all nations . . . Teaching them to observe all things whatsoever I have commanded you" (Matt. 28:19, 20).

Error and Truth at War in the Church

The basis of a true relationship with Jesus is obedience to all His commandments: "Ye are my friends, if ye do whatsoever I command you" (John 15:14).

Not only does the Bible call us to obedience but the Spirit of Prophecy also admonishes us to remain faithful. Following are a number of statements from Ellen White regarding the message of truth:

"Make your complaint, plainly and openly, in the right spirit, to the proper ones. Send in your petitions for things to be adjusted and set in order; but do not withdraw from the work of God, and prove unfaithful, because others are not doing right" (*Testimonies for the Church*, vol. 9, p. 249).

"My message to you is: No longer consent to listen without protest to the perversion of truth. Unmask the pretentious sophistries which, if received, will lead ministers and physicians and medical missionary workers to ignore the truth. Every one is now to stand on his guard. . . . I have been instructed to warn our people; for many are in danger of receiving theories and sophistries that undermine the foundation pillars of the faith" (*Selected Messages*, bk. 1, p. 196).

"The very last deception of Satan will be to make of none effect the testimony of the Spirit of God. 'Where there is no vision, the people perish' (Proverbs 29:18). Satan will work ingeniously, in different ways and through different agencies, to unsettle the confidence of God's remnant people in the true testimony" (*Selected Messages*, bk. 1, p. 48).

"The enemy has made his masterly efforts to unsettle the faith of our own people in the Testimonies . . . This is just as Satan designed it should be, and those who have been preparing the way for the people to pay no heed to the warnings and reproofs of the Testimonies of the Spirit of God will see that a tide of errors of all kinds will spring into life" (*Selected Messages*, bk. 3, p. 83).

"One thing is certain: Those Seventh-day Adventists who take their stand under Satan's banner will first give up their faith in the warnings and reproofs contained in the Testimonies of God's Spirit" (*Selected Messages*, bk. 3, p. 84).

"It is Satan's plan to weaken the faith of God's people in the *Testimonies*. Next follows skepticism in regard to the vital points of our faith, the pillars of our position, then doubt as to the Holy Scriptures, and then the downward march to perdition. When the *Testimonies*, which were once believed, are doubted and given up, Satan knows the deceived ones will not stop at this; and he redoubles his efforts till he launches them into open rebellion, which becomes incurable and ends in destruction" (*Testimonies for the Church*, vol. 4, p. 211).

Have we come to a point where we have given up Ellen White's writings, all her reproofs that God has so graciously given us? Has our condition now become "incurable"? If we still believe in all scriptures, what must we do in our local churches when we see the Word of God misused and error taught and practiced? Must we remain silent to keep peace and unity? Before we take the route of silence, let us examine five implications of silence.

First, we betray our sacred trust if we remain silent (2 Tim. 4:1-5). In our time, sound doctrine is not popular. People not led by the Holy Spirit are turning away their ears from the truth to fables. Before

Error and Truth at War in the Church

probation closes, we must be instant in season and out of season, reproving and rebuking and doing the work of an evangelist, or else God cannot use us and the devil will occupy us.

Second, we expose others to danger if we remain silent, as we are spiritual watchmen over Zion (Eze. 33:6, 7). As watchmen, day and night, we have a duty: "I have set watchmen upon thy walls, O Jerusalem, which shall never hold their peace day nor night: ye that make mention of the LORD, keep not silence" (Isa. 62:6). If we remain silent, we become "dumb dogs" that cannot bark to warn people of spiritual dangers (Isa. 56:10). Any minister who ignores the sin creeping into our church today and, instead of rebuking sin, preaches smooth sermons is not a true watchman.

Third, we are cursed if we remain silent (Judges 5:23). Ellen White stated: "If God abhors one sin above another, of which His people are guilty, it is doing nothing in case of an emergency. Indifference and neutrality in a religious crisis is regarded of God as a grievous crime and equal to the very worst type of hostility against God" (*Testimonies for the Church*, vol. 3, p. 280). Our duty to God demands that we remain not silent for the sake of unity when the people are led in error.

Fourth, the stones will cry out if we remain silent (Luke 19:40) or babes will speak for God (Ps. 8:2). Who knows if we have come to know the truth for such a time like this (Esther 4:14)? We must not remain silent.

Fifth, we ought to obey God rather than man (Acts 5:27-29) or church policies, and therefore, we have all reason not to be silent. The four lepers felt that if they remained silent punishment would overtake them (2 Kings 7:9). A true remnant must "no longer consent to listen without protest to the perversion of truth" (Ellen G. White, *Selected Messages*, bk. 1, p. 196). A watchman over Zion must not be silent!

Saints, many things have crept into our church that neither has any support from the Bible nor from the Spirit of Prophecy. Most of these

Awakening the Remnant

things that are very questionable, yet we either know not their basis or we fear to question lest we are labelled "he that troubleth Israel" (1 Kings 18:17).

Take for instance prayer trees where written pieces of prayers are hung on the tree and placed inside the sanctuary, take prayer walks, take our usual standing in worship prayer as opposed to kneeling (see Luke 22:41 and *Prophets and Kings,* p. 48), take prayer circles, take music of prayer where each individual prays aloud, causing confusion in the congregation. Where in the Bible or Spirit of Prophecy do we get these ideas? Take dancing in the worship service, the custom of celebrating members' birthdays during the worship service, the idea of giving awards or appreciation to politicians or clergy of other churches during our Sabbath worship service. These activities divert our attention to man and give him the glory that is due to God our Creator. Again, where in the Bible or in the Spirit of Prophecy are these ideas supported? Is God not particular about how we worship Him?

Are these things not coming from other churches? Biblically, we have but two churches represented by two women: the true church, the saints of Jesus (Rev. 12:1), and the false churches represented by the mother of harlots or Babylon (Rev. 17:3-6). We commit spiritual adultery or fornication when we pattern after false churches. Unless we distinguish between error and truth, rejecting error and holding unto truth, "we are in danger of becoming a sister to fallen Babylon, of allowing our churches to become corrupted, and filled with every foul spirit, a cage for every unclean and hateful bird; and will we be clear unless we make decided movements to cure the existing evil?" (Ellen G. White, *Testimonies on Sexual Behavior, Adultery, and Divorce,* p. 188).

Error and truth must not coexist in our church if we are to remain the pure church of Jesus Christ, the saints Jesus is coming back for. As Babylon makes "all nations drink of the wine of the wrath of her

Error and Truth at War in the Church

fornication" (Rev. 14:8), we the remnant church are to shout, "saying, Come out of her, my people, that ye be not partakers of her sins, and that ye receive not of her plagues" (Rev. 18:4). Ours is not a mission to mix error and truth.

What must faithful members concerned about questionable policies and doctrines in the church do? Should they leave the church? No! Never should any member for any reason ever leave the church. We are told: "Although there are evils existing in the church, and will be until the end of the world, the church in these last days is to be the light of the world that is polluted and demoralized by sin. The church, enfeebled and defective, needing to be reproved, warned, and counseled, is the only object upon earth upon which Christ bestows His supreme regard" (Ellen G. White, *Testimonies to Ministers and Gospel Workers*, p. 49). The saints are sealed while in church (Eze. 9:4). However, if you chose one Sabbath to worship with another Seventh-day Adventist church other than your local one, that should not be regarded as leaving the church.

So what do we do if we must not leave the church? Should we join in and practice questionable policies that conflict with the Bible? No! We are told: "God will have a people upon the earth to maintain the Bible, and the Bible only, as the standard of all doctrines and the basis of all reforms. The opinions of learned men, the deductions of science, the creeds or decisions of ecclesiastical councils, as numerous and discordant as are the churches which they represent, the voice of the majority,—not one or all of these should be regarded as evidence for or against any point of religious faith. Before accepting any doctrine or precept, we should demand a plain 'Thus saith the Lord' in its support" (Ellen G. White, *The Great Controversy*, p. 595). Like the Christians at Berea (Acts 17:10, 11), we should subject every church policy and teaching of men on our pulpits to the Scripture, and when

Awakening the Remnant

we detect error, we must not be silent, lest the blood of those who will be lost in error be required of us.

If in a particular local Seventh-day Adventist church, a minister chooses to promote practices that are not supported by either the Bible or the Spirit of Prophecy, we should prayerfully seek to help that minister. If we prayerfully reach out with a touch of truth and are rejected, we ought to prayerfully wait upon the Lord, as we ourselves remain pure from the errors. God gives to ministers the responsibility to feed the flock, and "if these in turn do not purify their lives from every wrong action, if they do not establish pure and holy principles in all their borders, then the Lord will grievously afflict and humble them and, unless they repent, will remove them from their place and make them a reproach" (Ellen G. White, *The Upward Look*, p. 131).

Ask yourself, if Paul were a member of my local synagogue, while remaining a Seventh-day Adventist, and he taught and persuaded all to follow the truth, but they refused, cast him out, and embraced error and vain worship, what would God have Paul do? We read of Paul in Acts 19:8-9: "And he went into the synagogue, and spake boldly for the space of three months, disputing and persuading the things concerning the kingdom of God. But when divers were hardened, and believed not, but spake evil of that way before the multitude, he departed from them, and separated the disciples, disputing daily in the school of one Tyrannus." True remnants will follow Paul's example where necessary.

As you pray for truth to prevail over errors, always pray for our ministers—a sacred trust is placed in their hands to prepare the church of Jesus. But all of us have a duty to work with ministers to nurture the church. "Those who have too little courage to reprove wrong, or who through indolence or lack of interest make no earnest effort to purify the family or the church of God, are held accountable for the evil that may result from their neglect of duty. We are just as responsible for

Error and Truth at War in the Church

evils that we might have checked in others by exercise of parental or pastoral authority as if the acts had been our own" (Ellen G. White, *Conflict and Courage*, p. 141).

While God calls pastors and laymen to work together, unconverted and corrupt pastors will set souls against God's message presented by laymen like the old reformation periods: "The fact that the message was, to a great extent, preached by laymen, was urged as an instrument against it. As of old, the plain testimony of God's Word was met with the inquiry, 'Have any of the rulers or of the Pharisees believed?' And finding how difficult a task it was to refute the arguments drawn from the prophetic periods, many discouraged the study of the prophecies, teaching that the prophetic books were sealed, and were not to be understood. Multitudes, trusting implicitly to their pastors, refused to listen to the warning; and others, though convinced of the truth, dared not confess it, lest they should be 'put out of the synagogue.' The message which God had sent for the testing and purification of the church, revealed all too surely how great was the number who had set their affections on this world rather than upon Christ" (Ellen G. White, *The Great Controversy*, p. 380).

To these corrupting influences, presentation of present truth is perceived as an attack on church leadership. Efforts are then placed on censoring truth and silencing messengers of truth. Saints, if you are disfellowshipped for awakening to the present truth, remember, "Blessed are ye, when men shall revile you, and persecute you, and shall say all manner of evil against you falsely, for my sake" (Matt. 5:11). Jesus tells us, "If they have persecuted me, they will also persecute you; if they have kept my saying, they will keep yours also" (John 15:20). And Paul tells us, "Stand therefore, having your loins girt about with truth" (Eph. 6:14).

Chapter 2

Amusements and Secular Dressing

With even greater force, the great controversy that began in heaven has stayed the course on the question of worship. Members of the Seventh-day Adventist Church may deny direct devil worship, but Satan knows that as long as we are kept amused by the world's entertainment industry and dress like the world's whores, while we claim to worship a true God, Satan will still be worshiped indirectly. Secularism in dress and amusements of this world have overtaken us, ministers and members alike, so that we see nothing wrong with this newfound friendship with the world. We have forgotten that "whosoever therefore will be a friend of the world is the enemy of God" (James 4:4). In regards to amusement, many of us are deceived by what we perceive as biblical silence on modern popular amusements.

The Bible speaks to us clearly concerning all things, either in detail or in principles. We take many things around us for granted; we count them as normal. There are many things that are deeply ingrained in our society that we need to consider anew. Amusements are one aspect of our secular society that, unfortunately, many church members within the remnant church fail to see the negative effects of in developing a heavenly character fit for the sealing before the close of

Awakening the Remnant

probation. Dress is another area where we have made no difference with the world. We will examine amusements first.

As God's people, we carry an end-time message to give to the world. We must act and talk with a Christ-like mind. In 1 Corinthians 13:11 we read: "When I was a child, I spake as a child, I understood as a child, I thought as a child: but when I became a man, I put away childish things."

The world today has gone mad with grown-up men doing "childish things" in sports. Take Rugby for example, where grown men run up and down on what looks like a cow pasture, throwing what looks like a pig's bladder to each other to cross a goal line and then kicking that pig's bladder through what looks like two gold posts. Even members of the remnant church find these "childish things" entertaining, with worldly audience not really caring what the "children" on the field really do. The audience just wants to get drunk, yell, scream, curse, and take the Lord's name in vain.

We are called to put away "childish things" and be Christ-like. To do that, we have to have a renewed mind. Romans 12:2 tells us, "And be not conformed to this world: but be ye transformed by the renewing of your mind, that ye may prove what is that good, and acceptable, and perfect, will of God." Is it a minor issue to write on this subject?

When we sit in our living room before our television sets to watch world games, we forget that God has a panoramic view. These games, invented by Satan, are ensnaring the world into vainglory. God watches the drunken throng on the football field; the vulgar language used by the football fans, taking God's name in vain; the drugs used; the fornication involved; the precious soul winning time wasted; and all the effects on the entire human race these games create. God watches, as if powerless to stop His remnants from getting involved. He watches His holy angels stand aside as His children are amused by these inventions of Satan who once sought to derail Jesus from paying the

Amusements and Secular Dressing

cost of our salvation. Angels holding the four winds begin to let go. Jesus, watching the remnant glued to television screens, cries to God the Father, "My blood, My blood, My blood!" Is it a minor issue to write on this? Is it not God's love to call us through this book to urgent repentance?

Among the principles of Christian behavior presented in the Bible is a special care for how and what we do since this impacts what we become. We notice the counsel of Paul: "Let nothing be done through strife or vainglory; but in lowliness of mind let each esteem other better than themselves" (Phil. 2:3). The passage continues by showing how Jesus voluntarily descended from the glories of heaven to the humble state of fallen humanity. In verse 7, Jesus "made Himself of no reputation."

Jesus emptied Himself of His divine power. He is our example. He relied upon no power we ourselves cannot access. Now we, like Him, must empty ourselves and be acquainted with Him who made Himself of no reputation. But the trend of sports is anything but making oneself of no reputation! It is very difficult to see how having the mind of Christ can mesh with having the mind of an athlete bent upon defeating his foe through strength of might and through various plays that trick your opponent.

We find nowhere in Scripture any slightest hint from Jesus that He would have us feed the kind of nature in sports that inclines us to selfishness. Read the following verses:

"Whosoever shall exalt himself shall be abased; and he that shall humble himself shall be exalted" (Matt. 23:12).

"Whosoever will be great among you, let him be your minister; And whosoever will be chief among you, let him be your servant: Even as the Son of man came not to be ministered

Awakening the Remnant

unto, but to minister, and to give his life a ransom for many" (Matt. 20:26-28).

"For he that is least among you all, the same shall be great" (Luke 9:48).

A peculiar people, a true Seventh-day Adventist, would have a difficult time competing if he held to the Christ-like philosophy of humility outlined in Scripture. In all sports, whether it be the so-called church sports widely practiced in our Seventh-day Adventist schools, there is always a winner, and there is always a loser. But in the Christ-like view, all who strive for God's will can win; there need be no losers. There is a fundamental disconnect between the gospel of God and the philosophy of sports. Following the words of Jesus in Luke 9:48, being "least among you all" would result in a poor showing in sports.

Some may pose a question: what about Paul's use of imagery borrowed from Grecian sporting competitions? Others may insist that we can develop "a philosophy of sport" on the basis of such texts. Rather than condemn such minds, let us put this "to the law and to the testimony" (Isa. 8:20) and see if that holds any truth.

First, we turn to 1 Corinthians 9:24-27: "Know ye not that they which run in a race run all, but one receiveth the prize? So run, that ye may obtain. And every man that striveth for the mastery is temperate in all things. Now they do it to obtain a corruptible crown; but we an incorruptible. I therefore so run, not as uncertainly; so fight I, not as one that beateth the air: But I keep under my body, and bring it into subjection: lest that by any means, when I have preached to others, I myself should be a castaway."

How do you read that? Paul points out the giant cleavage, the great contrast between the Grecian competition and the Christian life. Many run in a Grecian competitive footrace, but there is only one

Amusements and Secular Dressing

winner. Like a race, there is something to be obtained at the end of the Christian pathway. We, too, are to be active so that we may successfully obtain that. But in what particular way are we to be active? As the runners strive for mastery, they engage in a careful, temperate lifestyle to reach peak performance. And if they win, what do they receive? A corruptible crown. What do we in the Christian walk receive? An incorruptible crown. In other words, the contrast is between a temporal victory as passing as the wind and an eternal result in value beyond measure. Paul is not promoting sports at all.

In fact, Paul insists that he is not running uncertainly; he is not competing for a prize that, odds are, he is unlikely to obtain. With the value of the prize before him in mind, Paul runs; he fights; he exercises self-discipline. He is very alert to the necessity of maintaining control over the sinful nature. He knows that it is ever ready to rise up and express itself in evil poured out of us and into the world, shaming our Christian witness for God. And so Paul, by analogy of a sportsman, strives daily to surrender his will to the Lordship of Jesus Christ our Savior, until he can say, "I am crucified with Christ: nevertheless I live; yet not I, but Christ liveth in me: and the life which I now live in the flesh I live by the faith of the Son of God, who loved me, and gave Himself for me" (Gal. 2:20).

This surely is the correct reading of Paul' writing. There is nothing in this passage upon which we can build up an artificial philosophy of sports. The whole thrust of Paul's argument is that if even the worldly person is willing to go to such great lengths to obtain a temporary crown that wilts, how much more should the saints of God strive to live out the fullness of Christianity! There is no advocacy here for a remnant of God to participate in sports. A lesson is being drawn from a worldly practice and used in the context of a letter written to a church composed mostly of people from the Greek culture that are very familiar with the surrounding culture of sports. That is all.

Awakening the Remnant

We now turn to Paul's use of Hebrews 12:1 and 2: "Wherefore seeing we also are compassed about with so great a cloud of witnesses, let us lay aside every weight, and the sin which doth so easily beset us, and let us run with patience the race that is set before us, Looking unto Jesus the author and finisher of our faith; who for the joy that was set before him endured the cross, despising the shame, and is set down at the right hand of the throne of God."

Here, Paul likens the remnant's journey to a running race, although this time to an audience that is predominantly Jewish. He points to the victory of Christ at the cross, and our part as well, our patient running of the race, our steadfast striving to surrender our will to the Lordship of Christ so that we gain His power to lay aside every sin. He shows us that our eyes must focus on the finish line—Christ-likeness. He points to Christ's suffering, not to obtain an earthly crown, but eternal life for the believer. The suffering of Christ is put in the center rather than the suffering of the remnant as he participates in the journey home.

In the same passage, Paul refers to the cloud of witnesses spoken of in Hebrews 11—those who have breasted the evils and difficulties in their way and who in the name of the Lord have braced themselves successfully against the opposing forces of evil. We, too, must now magnify the truth before the world and other witnesses watching us. Again, the goal here is one that involves a moral imperative, the renunciation of sin, and an eternal reward for the believer. There is nothing here to create a philosophy of sports from. The remnant must be active; we must actively submit to God so that sin may be put away. No advocacy of participation in trickery and aggression of sports can be found here.

By analogy of what Paul is teaching by use of imagery, Ellen White also tells us of the battle we have to fight. She says: "The Christian life is a battle and a march. In this warfare there is no release; the effort must be continuous and persevering. It is by unceasing endeavor

Amusements and Secular Dressing

that we maintain the victory over the temptations of Satan. Christian integrity must be sought with resistless energy and maintained with a resolute fixedness of purpose" (*The Ministry of Healing*, p. 453).

In your further study, you will find that the same spiritual meaning applies to other texts that use cultural imagery. These texts include Galatians 2:2 and 5:7, 2 Timothy 2:5 and 4:7, and Philippians 3:13 and 14. Read these texts prayerfully to discern the truth.

A usage of images from Grecian athletic competitions in some illustrations is no license or library from which to develop a "philosophy of sports." We can no more create a philosophy of sports than we can develop a philosophy of adultery, a philosophy of car theft, or a philosophy of murder. Remember, the physical must be kept in harmony with the spiritual or else our character will not be truly transformed to Christ-likeness but instead harmonize with the world to perish through sports.

A closer examination reveals that the nature of sports wars against the Spirit of God. In Galatians 5:22 and 23 we read: "But the fruit of the Spirit is love, joy, peace, longsuffering, gentleness, goodness, faith, Meekness, temperance: against such there is no law." We find nowhere in Scripture any room for the type of mindset that spurs a remnant to compete against and prevail over someone else, to also bring forth the fruit of the Spirit as recorded in Galatians. When examining these fruit, with a Spirit of God, we have to come to the conclusion that the beautiful fruit that God expects to grow in us, for the glory of our Lord Jesus Christ, as we divorce ourselves from the world and its lusts, are at serious war with the bitter and poisonous fruits that are produced in a life that continues to be influenced by trickery and aggression that is common to sports.

We are running the race, not of earthly things, but of spiritual. We dare not succumb to false scholarships that are damaging to our heavenly character development. We dare not push our young people

Awakening the Remnant

into participation in such operations. They have enough challenges without us pushing them into this pit. We dare not make the physical misshapen and put it in opposition to the spiritual. Those who are under the training of God reveal a life that is not in harmony with the world, its customs, or its practices. That is where we need to stand. Amusements may have a ubiquitous place in society, but it is not so firmly entrenched that we must surrender the gospel of God. Let us beware of this insidious disease creeping into our midst, and let us reject altogether the concept of amusements. Let us be open to the guidance of the Holy Spirit in the remnant church.

Some may argue that it is only competitive sports that are to be shunned. Indeed, ministers and our institutions may argue so. But this is a very deceptive excuse, as most of our schools do compete, count scores, declare winners, and collect sports awards. Moreover, this argument has no scriptural basis—no Bible and no Spirit of Prophecy basis. Others may argue that they watch or participate in sports for exercise. It is a lame excuse, for in watching games one does not exercise but self-amuse. Of course even ministers are active in sports to keep physically fit, and all this in the name of following counsel of God's prophet Ellen White about exercise. We can settle this argument by quoting Ellen White in *Fundamentals of Christian Education*: "I have not been able to find one instance where He educated His disciples to engage in amusement of football or pugilistic games, to obtain physical exercise, or in theatrical performances; and yet Christ was our pattern in all things" (p. 229).

Some scorn the above passage and say that football was not even played in Jesus' time. They miss the principle God is telling us through His prophet Ellen White. Moreover, a careful reading of Isaiah 22:18—"toss thee like a ball into a large country"—would suggest the ball game of some kind has been around longer than we may think. A game of some sort was played on Jesus when they covered His

Amusements and Secular Dressing

head with an old garment, blindfolding Him, and then struck Him in the face and cried out, "Prophesy unto us, thou Christ, Who is he that smote thee?" (Matt. 26:68). Many Greek games—boxing, wrestling, beast fights—were around during Jesus' time, yet He never partook of them.

The Holy Spirit through Ellen White is telling us that Jesus never "educated His disciples to engage in amusement of football or pugilistic games, to obtain physical exercise." Leave these games alone! So, how must we exercise? We need exercise and are use to exercising through games, you may say. If we are faithful in obeying the truth, it should never be based on finding alternatives to sports first. Truth should be obeyed for it being the truth. Those who fear God will never lack means outside sports to exercise.

Clearly, no true Seventh-day Adventist should participate or encourage the use of amusements prohibited in the principles of the Bible. These include playing cards, chess, football, tennis, cricket, baseball, croquet, and any other amusements of such category or that fall under the principles by which these are prohibited. We are a remnant church who keep the commandments of God and have the testimony of Jesus (Rev. 12:17), which testimony is the Spirit of Prophecy (Rev. 19:10). With Ellen White's writings, we have no excuse for engaging in sports. If we were any other church, we could humanly have argued that the Bible does not say that football or baseball should not be played. The faithful witness is plainly against us making any lame excuse. Let us consider these passages from the Spirit of Prophecy:

> "Love not the world, neither the things that are in the world. If any man love the world, the love of the Father is not in him. 1 John 2:15. The true Christian will not desire to enter any place of amusement or engage in any diversion upon which he cannot ask the blessing of God. He will not be found at the

theater, the billiard hall, or the bowling saloon. He will not unite with the gay waltzers, or indulge in any other bewitching pleasure that will banish Christ from the mind.

"To those who plead for these diversions, we answer, We cannot indulge in them in the name of Jesus of Nazareth.... Go in imagination to Gethsemane and behold the anguish which Christ endured for us. See the world's Redeemer wrestling in superhuman agony, the sins of the whole world upon His soul. Hear His prayer, borne upon the sympathizing breeze, 'O my Father, if it be possible, let this cup pass from me: nevertheless not as I will, but as thou wilt' (Matthew 26:39). The hour of darkness has come. Christ has entered the shadow of His cross. Alone He must drink the bitter cup. Of all earth's children whom He has blessed and comforted there is not one to console Him in this dreadful hour. He is betrayed into the hands of a murderous mob. Faint and weary, He is dragged from one tribunal to another.... He who knew not the taint of sin pours out His life as a malefactor upon Calvary. This history should stir every soul to its depths. It was to save us that the Son of God became a man of sorrows and acquainted with grief.... Let a sense of the infinite sacrifice made for our redemption be ever with you, and the ballroom will lose its attractions.

"Not only did Christ die as our sacrifice, but He lived as our example. In His human nature He stands, complete, perfect, spotless. To be a Christian is to be Christlike. Our entire being—soul, body, and spirit—must be purified, ennobled, sanctified, until we shall reflect His image and imitate His example.... We need not fear to engage in any pursuit or pleasure that will aid us in this work. But it is our duty to shun every-

Amusements and Secular Dressing

thing that would divert our attention or lessen our zeal" (*That I May Know Him*, p. 311).

"The mind thus educated to enjoy physical taxation in practical life becomes enlarged, and through culture and training, well disciplined and richly furnished for usefulness, and acquires a knowledge essential to be a help and blessing to themselves and to others. Let every student consider, and be able to say, I study, I work, for eternity. They can learn to be patiently industrious and persevering in their combined efforts of physical and mental labor. What force of powers is put into your games of football and your other inventions after the way of the Gentiles—exercises which bless no one! Just put the same powers into exercise in doing useful labor, and would not your record be more pleasing to meet in the great day of God?

"Whatever is done under the sanctified stimulus of Christian obligation, because you are stewards in trust of talents to use to be a blessing to yourself and to others, gives you substantial satisfaction; for all is done to the glory of God. I cannot find an instance in the life of Christ where He devoted time to play and amusement. He was the great Educator for the present and the future life. I have not been able to find one instance where He educated His disciples to engage in amusement of football or pugilistic games, to obtain physical exercise, or in theatrical performances; and yet Christ was our pattern in all things. Christ, the world's Redeemer, gave to every man his work and bids them 'occupy till I come.' And in doing His work, the heart warms to such an enterprise, and all the powers of the soul are enlisted in a work assigned of the Lord and Master. It is a high and important work. The Christian teacher and student are enabled to become stewards of the grace of Christ, and be always in earnest" (*Fundamentals of Christian Education*, p. 229).

"The public feeling is that manual labor is degrading, yet men may exert themselves as much as they choose at cricket, baseball, or in pugilistic contests, without being regarded as degraded. Satan is delighted when he sees human beings using their physical and mental powers in that which does not educate, which is not useful, which does not help them to be a blessing to those who need their help. While the youth are becoming expert in games that are of no real value to themselves or to others, Satan is playing the game of life for their souls. Taking from them the talents that God has given them, and placing in their stead his own evil attributes. It is his effort to lead men to ignore God. He seeks to engross and absorb the mind so completely that God will find no place in the thoughts. He does not wish people to have a knowledge of their Maker, and he is well pleased if he can set in operation games and theatrical performances that will so confuse the senses of the youth that God and heaven will be forgotten" (*Messages to Young People*, p. 213).

"The world is not a croquet ground, on which we are to amuse ourselves; it is a school where we are to study earnestly and thoroughly the lessons given in the word of God. There they may learn how to receive and how to impart. There they may learn how to seek for souls in the highways and byways of life. How earnestly the games of this world are engaged in! If those who engage in them would strive as earnestly for the crown of life which fadeth not away, what victories they

Amusements and Secular Dressing

would gain! They would become medical missionaries, and they would see how much they could do to relieve suffering humanity. What a blessing they would be! What we need is practical education. Ministers and people, practice the lessons Christ has given in His word, and you will become Christlike in character" (*Medical Ministry*, p. 318).

"The true Christian will not desire to enter any place of amusement or engage in any diversion upon which he cannot ask the blessing of God. He will not be found at the theater, the billiard hall, or the bowling saloon. He will not unite with the gay waltzers or indulge in any other bewitching pleasure that will banish Christ from the mind.

"To those who plead for these diversions we answer, We cannot indulge in them in the name of Jesus of Nazareth. The blessing of God would not be invoked upon the hour spent at the theater or in the dance. No Christian would wish to meet death in such a place. No one would wish to be found there when Christ shall come" (*The Adventist Home*, pp. 515, 516).

"Such an example makes an impression upon the minds of youth. They notice that lotteries and fairs and games are sanctioned by the church, and they think there is something fascinating in this way of obtaining means. A youth is surrounded by temptations. He enters the bowling alley, the gambling saloon, to see the sport. He sees the money taken by the one who wins. This looks enticing. It seems an easier way of obtaining money than by earnest work, which requires persevering energy and strict economy. He imagines there can be no harm in this; for similar games have been resorted to in order to obtain means for the benefit of the church. Then why should he not help himself in this way?" (*Counsels on Stewardship*, p. 201).

"Some of the most popular amusements, such as football and boxing, have become schools of brutality. They are developing the same characteristics as did the games of ancient Rome. The love of domination, the pride in mere brute force, the reckless disregard of life, are exerting upon the youth a power to demoralize that is appalling" (*The Adventist Home*, p. 500).

"God designs that the body shall be a temple for His Spirit. How solemn then is the responsibility resting on every soul.... How many there are, blessed with reason and intelligence, talents which should be used to the glory of God, who willfully degrade soul and body. Their lives are a continual round of excitement. Cricket and football matches and horse racing absorb the attention. The liquor curse, with its world of woe, is defiling the temple of God. . . . By the use of liquor and tobacco men are debasing the life given them for high and holy purposes. Their practices are represented by wood, hay, and stubble. Their God-given powers are perverted, their senses degraded, to minister to the desires of the carnal mind" (*Temperance*, p. 142).

"Every day there is housework to be done—cooking, washing dishes, sweeping, and dusting. Mothers, have you taught your daughters to do these daily duties? ... Their muscles need exercise. In the place of getting exercise by jumping and playing ball or croquet, let their exercise be to some purpose" (*Child Guidance*, p. 352).

Amusements and Secular Dressing

"Washing clothes upon the old-fashioned rubbing-board, sweeping, dusting, and a variety of other duties in the kitchen and the garden, will be valuable exercise for young ladies. Such useful labor will supply the place of croquet, archery, dancing, and other amusements which benefit no one" (*Fundamentals of Christian Education*, p. 74).

"No Day for Pleasure Seeking, Swimming, or Ball Playing.— God would have all His gifts appreciated. All fragments, jots, and tittles are to be treasured carefully, and we are carefully to become acquainted with the necessities of others. All that we have of Bible truth is not merely for our benefit, but to impart to other souls, and this is to be impressed upon human minds, and every kindly word spoken to prepare the way to make a channel through which the truth will flow forth in rich currents to other souls.

"Every working of Christ in miracles was essential, and was to reveal to the world that there was a great work to be done on the Sabbath day for the relief of suffering humanity, but the common work was not to be done. Pleasure seeking, ball playing, swimming, was not a necessity, but a sinful neglect of the sacred day sanctified by Jehovah. Christ did not perform miracles merely to display His power, but always to meet Satan in afflicting suffering humanity. Christ came to our world to meet the needs of the suffering, whom Satan was torturing" (*Selected Messages*, bk. 3, p. 258).

"The true followers of Christ will have sacrifices to make. They will shun places of worldly amusement because they find no Jesus there,—no influence which will make them heavenly minded and increase their growth in grace. Obedience to the word of God will lead them to come out from all these things, and be separate" (*Messages to Young People*, p. 376).

In matters of sports, it is with much sadness that most ministers and leaders in our institutions who read the above biblical and Spirit of Prophecy quotes may dismiss them as not relevant to modern times or simply ignore counsel to keep their institutions in line with world standards. To many, school ratings in the world are more important than following the plain Word of God. These leaders speak from pulpits and steer the train with the remnants on board. But more fearful is the thought that Satan knows that as long as the remnant church is amused in these games, they cannot develop a perfect heavenly character, they will not be sealed, they will end up worshiping the beast, and eventually Satan will claim victory over them in the great controversy.

Before we turn to secularisation in dress, we must not be silent about objectionable use of television sets in most of our living rooms. One question we ought to ask is how much spiritual empowerment can a true remnant obtain out of watching a show on a television set? We commonly argue for having a television set in our living rooms to use it as an educational tool for the family. But how often the lust of the eyes lures us beyond the boundaries! Most, if not all programs, even the most educational documentaries, do not build our characters for the sealing before the close of probation.

Evil is all around us in the streets of most cities, and we struggle to turn away from the enticing scenes of evil we cannot avoid while walking down the street. We have enough temptation to occupy all of our time and effort without bringing a deliberate source of temptation right into the living room. The Lord through His prophet—Ellen White—has repeatedly warned against the likes of bowling and going to movie theaters. We must apply the same warnings to movies

Amusements and Secular Dressing

we watch in our living rooms. The devil would have us think that the Lord is only against watching a movie in the theater, and the movie becomes a "Christian movie" once bought for family use in the living room.

World TV programs are not produced by people who have come in the spirit of Elijah or John the Baptist to prepare us for the sealing. No wonder Satan manipulates the effects of these scenes. Most of our senses have been damned over the years of abuse with what the world offers us through TV, that we have come to rationalize snatches and phrases of gutter talk that creep into most educational shows as innocent. The often-short clips of immoral acts that appear in TV documentaries, we have come to rationalize as acceptable innocent looks.

We fail to detect how this innocent look is a sin. We fail to trace back in history the innocent looks of our mother Eve in the Garden of Eden. Her innocent looks on the forbidden tree led into all the multiplied sorrows and eventual deaths of billions of human beings over six tragic millenniums. We fail to trace back in history the innocent looks of King David. He awoke from an afternoon nap and coincidently saw his neighbor's beautiful wife taking a bath on her Mediterranean roof garden. His innocent looks led to adultery and murder, sins that influenced a whole nation to forget God. The results of King David's immorality with Bathsheba so marked the family of David that four of his own children were taken from him by tragedy or apostasy. How bitterly he later lamented the scarring consequences of his innocent looking. We must not set up our minds, which are already overwhelmed with sinful thoughts, for avoidable assaults of the enemy through so-called innocent looks at evil on our television screens.

Jesus tells us, "Ye have heard that it was said of them of old time, Thou shalt not commit adultery: But I say unto you, That whosoever looketh on a woman to lust after her hath committed adultery with her already in his heart" (Matt. 5:27, 28). Our creator, the wise Jesus, is

Awakening the Remnant

simply telling us the science of our wonderfully made beings: since the brain is the decision center for the body, every act performed must first be conceived in the mind before it can be translated into action.

To our movies on TV, Jesus is simply telling us that by beholding we become changed and that we vicariously participate in the actual act. Even though the viewer may be mature enough to know that the scene is only a fabricated, pretend situation, he becomes as emotionally involved in the picture as if he were actually living out the experience. The heart pounds with fright, the eyes fill with tears, and the viewer mentally projectd himself into the movie scene. Whether fighting and shooting his way out of a desperate situation, suffering the trauma of incurable disease, addicting to immoral habits, or yielding to the excitement of a provocative bedroom scene, the viewer is caught up in the plot, taking part by proxy in the adventures of the hero or heroine. Jesus said that this kind of participation is just as wrong as the actual physical involvement in sin.

Jesus tells us the solution to the lusts of the eye: "And if thy right eye offend thee, pluck it out, and cast it from thee: for it is profitable for thee that one of thy members should perish, and not that thy whole body should be cast into hell" (Matt. 5:29). If we apply the principle to our TV viewing, Jesus is saying that if the eye is looking at a movie that is liable to lead the mind to harbor sin, the most drastic action should be taken to put those scenes out of view. Jesus is saying here that if we have a TV set in the home which we cannot control, it is better to cast it out of the house onto the junk pile than to be led into sin by its influence. Better to lead a so-called one-eyed existence without television than to lose our soul by defiling, sinful thoughts created by it. The only way to be pure minded is to look at, listen to, and speak only the things that are pure.

Paul tells us: "Finally, brethren, whatsoever things are true, whatsoever things are honest, whatsoever things are just, whatsoever things

Amusements and Secular Dressing

are pure, whatsoever, things are lovely, whatsoever things are of good report; if there be any virtue, and if there be any praise, think on these things" (Phil. 4:8). The secret of being pure, honest, and virtuous is to think that way, and the way we think is determined by what we see, hear and speak. Saints, let us learn from the lessons King David learned and say, "I will set no wicked thing before mine eyes" (Ps. 101:3).

As to secularisation in dress, we must understand as remnants, there is a limit to how we should dress in comparison to the secular world. We are first and foremost told: "Wherefore come out from among them, and be ye separate, saith the Lord" (2 Cor. 6:17). Our outward dress is a measure of our inward dress. The Spirit of Prophecy tells us: "A person's character is judged by his style of dress. A refined taste, a cultivated mind, will be revealed in the choice of simple and appropriate attire" (*Education*, p. 248).

As God's children, we are to maintain a distinction from the ways of inhabitants of this world. We read from 2 Corinthians 6:14-18 that the love of Christ constrains us from reaching out after the lusts of the flesh. As such, we know that "Christ's followers are required to come out from the world, and be separate, and touch not the unclean, and they have the promise of being the sons and daughters of the Most High, members of the royal family. But if the conditions are not complied with on their part, they will not, cannot, realize the fulfillment of the promise. A profession of Christianity is nothing in the sight of God; but true, humble, willing obedience to His requirements designates the children of His adoption" (Ellen G. White, *Testimonies for the Church*, vol. 2, p. 441).

Ellen White also wrote, "God will have a people separate and distinct from the world. And as soon as any have a desire to imitate the fashions of the world, that they do not immediately subdue, just so soon God ceases to acknowledge them as His children. They are the children of the world and of darkness. They lust for the leeks and onions of Egypt, that is, desire to be as much like the world as possible; by so doing, those that profess to have put on Christ virtually put Him off, and show that they are strangers to grace and strangers to the meek and lowly Jesus. If they had acquainted themselves with Him, they would walk worthy of Him" (*Testimonies for the Church*, vol. 1, p. 136).

For every requirement, God has a good purpose for us. In choosing the dress of the Israelites, God intended to remind the Israelites of their salvation (Num. 15:38-41). In Numbers 15:40 we read: "That ye may remember, and do all my commandments, and be holy unto your God."

We are told by Ellen White that "God expressly commanded a very simple arrangement of dress for the children of Israel for the purpose of distinguishing them from the idolatrous nations around them. As they looked upon their peculiarity of dress, they were to remember that they were God's commandment-keeping people, and that He had wrought in a miraculous manner to bring them from Egyptian bondage to serve Him, to be a holy people unto Him. They were not to serve their own desires, or to imitate the idolatrous nations around them, but to remain a distinct, separate people, that all who looked upon them might say: These are they whom God brought out of the land of Egypt, who keep the law of Ten Commandments. An Israelite was known to be such as soon as seen, for God through simple means distinguished him as His" (*Testimonies for the Church*, vol. 1, p. 524).

We must understand the factors that should guide us in our choice of dress. We read in Exodus 23:2: "Thou shalt not follow a multitude to do evil; neither shalt thou speak in a cause to decline after many to wrest judgment."

We are told by Ellen White that "Christians should not take pains to make themselves gazing-stocks by dressing differently from the

Amusements and Secular Dressing

world. But if, in accordance with their faith and duty in respect to their dressing modestly and healthfully, they find themselves out of fashion, they should not change their dress in order to be like the world. But they should manifest a noble independence and moral courage to be right, if all the world differs from them. If the world introduces a modest, convenient, and healthful mode of dress, which is in accordance with the Bible, it will not change our relation to God or to the world to adopt such a style of dress. Christians should follow Christ, and conform their dress to God's word. They should shun extremes. They should humbly pursue a straight-forward course, irrespective of applause or of censure, and should cling to the right because of its own merits" (*Messages to Young People*, p. 350). She further wrote: "Fashion is deteriorating the intellect and eating out the spirituality of our people" (*Testimonies for the Church*, vol. 4, p. 647).

God alone can read our hearts, but our dress allows man to have a glimpse of what is inside us. If we change inside, then the dress must change to reflect that purity in us. As such, whatever we do must be for God's glory (1 Cor. 10:31) lest we bring shame on God. We must adorn from the heart with meekness and quiet spirit that reflects the high price Jesus paid to redeem us (1 Peter 3:3-5). We must not adorn with costly array, but with modest apparel that professes godliness with good works (1 Tim. 2:9, 10).

If our hearts are not renewed, our dress will show, for "a person's character is judged by his style of dress. A refined taste, a cultivated mind, will be revealed in the choice of simple and appropriate attire. Chaste simplicity in dress, when united with modesty of demeanor, will go far toward surrounding a young woman with that atmosphere of sacred reserve which will be to her a shield from a thousand perils" (Ellen G. White, *Education*, p. 248).

We are told by Ellen White that "the dress and its arrangement upon the person is generally found to be the index of the man or the woman. We judge of a person's character by the style of dress worn. A modest, godly woman will dress modestly. A refined taste, a cultivated mind, will be revealed in the choice of a simple, appropriate attire" (*Child Guidance*, p. 413).

The other factor we should consider when choosing our dress is health. We read in 3 John 2: "Beloved, I wish above all things that thou mayest prosper and be in health, even as thy soul prospereth." Certain clothes, say tight dresses and those that expose limbs, may cause health problems. We are told: "Satan is constantly devising some new style of dress that shall prove an injury to physical and moral health; and he exults when he sees professed Christians eagerly accepting the fashions that he has invented. The amount of physical suffering created by unnatural and unhealthful dress cannot be estimated. Many have become lifelong invalids through their compliance with the demands of fashion" (Ellen G. White, *Counsels on Health*, p. 599).

More specifically talking about exposure of body limbs, the wise man observed: "She is not afraid of the snow for her household: for all her household are clothed with scarlet" (Prov. 31:21). We are told in the Spirit of Prophecy that "Satan invented the fashions which leave the limbs exposed, chilling back the life current from its original course. And parents bow at the shrine of fashion and so clothe their children that the nerves and veins become contracted, and do not answer the purpose that God designed they should. The result is habitually cold feet and hands. Those parents who follow fashion instead of reason will have an account to render to God for thus robbing their children of health. Even life itself is frequently sacrificed to the god of fashion" (*Child Guidance,* p. 427).

The most objectionable part of dressing like the world, for which the majority of those who profess to be a part of the remnants are guilty, is wearing clothes that pertain to the opposite sex. God was explicit on this: "The woman shall not wear that which pertaineth unto a

Amusements and Secular Dressing

man, neither shall a man put on a woman's garment: for all that do so are abomination unto the LORD thy God" (Deut. 22:5). Man has since sought to rationalize and justify deviating from God's instruction.

For the remnants, God spoke again in the Spirit of Prophecy: "There is an increasing tendency to have women in their dress and appearance as near like the other sex as possible, and to fashion their dress very much like that of men, but God pronounces it abomination. 'In like manner also, that women adorn themselves in modest apparel, with shamefacedness and sobriety.' 1 Timothy 2:9. Those who feel called out to join the movement in favor of woman's rights and the so-called dress reform might as well sever all connection with the third angel's message. The spirit which attends the one cannot be in harmony with the other. The Scriptures are plain upon the relations and rights of men and women" (*Testimonies for the Church*, vol. 1, p. 457).

It is very unfortunate that new converts are often not taught principles of dress. The first principle is to bear good fruit, for it is by our fruits shown through our dress that we are to be known (Matt. 7:16-20). To bear good fruit, we are required to come out of world fashions and be "separate," then we can be "sons and daughters" of our God (2 Cor. 6:17, 18). How these principles of "fruit" and being "separate" apply to dress must be taught to new converts.

We are told: "One of the points upon which those newly come to the faith will need instruction is the subject of dress. Let the new converts be faithfully dealt with. Are they vain in dress? Do they cherish pride of heart? The idolatry of dress is a moral disease. It must not be taken over into the new life. In most cases, submission to the gospel requirements will demand a decided change in the dress" (Ellen G. White, *Testimonies for the Church*, vol. 6, p. 96).

Being separate from the world in dress fashions must be taught to new converts before they are baptized, otherwise we give room for Satan to plant tares. We are told: "Baptism is a most solemn renun-

Awakening the Remnant

ciation of the world. Those who are baptized in the threefold name of the Father, the Son, and the Holy Spirit, at the very entrance of their Christian life declare publicly that they have forsaken the service of Satan and have become members of the royal family, children of the heavenly King. They have obeyed the command: 'Come out from among them, and be ye separate, ... and touch not the unclean thing.' And to them is fulfilled the promise: 'I will receive you, and will be a Father unto you, and ye shall be My sons and daughters, saith the Lord Almighty.' 2 Corinthians 6:17, 18" (Ellen G. White, *Testimonies for the Church*, vol. 6, p. 91).

After the taught and baptized member continues to follow the fashions of the world, the church needs to act in a manner that is loving, and yet not compromising with sin. The principles are laid out in the Bible. In 1 Corinthians 5:1-13, Paul is uncompromising on how we should deal with open sins—which dress fits. We must "purge out therefore the old leaven, that ye may be a new lump" and "put away from among yourselves that wicked person." This includes censure and disfellowship actions of the church. This is tough but inspired language.

However, we often play with sin in the church. In 2 Corinthians 2:1-11 Paul labors to explain that it was out of love that he first wrote to the church with "heaviness" for he had written "out of much affliction and anguish of heart" and "with much tears" due to the sin in the church, but even this time, the tried apostle did not forget to require them to "be obedient in all things." In 1 Timothy 5:20 Paul is again uncompromising. This time he instructed young Timothy, saying, "Them that sin rebuke before all, that others also may fear." Certain sin needs open rebuke. It is OK to say to a sister, "That is inappropriate dress (or lack of dress) for church."

Ellen White wrote, "Obedience to fashion is pervading our Seventh-day Adventist churches and is doing more than any other power

Amusements and Secular Dressing

to separate our people from God. I have been shown that our church rules are very deficient. All exhibitions of pride in dress, which is forbidden in the word of God, should be sufficient reason for church discipline. If there is a continuance, in face of warnings and appeals and entreaties, to still follow the perverse will, it may be regarded as proof that the heart is in no way assimilated to Christ. Self, and only self, is the object of adoration, and one such professed Christian will lead many away from God.

"There is a terrible sin upon us as a people, that we have permitted our church members to dress in a manner inconsistent with their faith. We must arise at once and close the door against the allurements of fashion. Unless we do this, our churches will become demoralized" (*Testimonies for the Church*, vol. 4, pp. 647, 648).

We must not ever think that disregarding deportment in dress has no consequences. For those women who wear trousers fashioned after men's trousers, both the Bible and the Spirit of Prophecy clearly call both the dress and the person an abomination. We may make all the arguments about what the Bible and the Spirit of Prophecy meant, we may relate to today's culture and acceptability, and we may argue that it is difficult in certain work places to discard trousers, but there is a cost of being a true remnant who must be sealed before the close of probation. You may even on this point denounce this book and find another author who will write what you wish to hear.

It is safer in all walks of life, in all places and circumstances, for sisters who are truly remnants to leave any resemblance of trousers alone! The Bible tells us the fate of those who follow fashion and disregard counsel on dress: "And there shall in no wise enter into it any thing that defileth, neither whatsoever worketh abomination, or maketh a lie: but they which are written in the Lamb's book of life" (Rev. 21:27).

Awakening the Remnant

Since it is our sisters who are affected on the question of dress, let me conclude by saying this, may the following inspired counsel speak to your heart:

"Do not, my sisters, trifle longer with your own souls and with God. I have been shown that the main cause of your backsliding is your love of dress. This leads to the neglect of grave responsibilities, and you find yourselves with scarcely a spark of the love of God in your hearts. Without delay, renounce the cause of your backsliding, because it is sin against your own soul and against God. Be not hardened by the deceitfulness of sin. Fashion is deteriorating the intellect and eating out the spirituality of our people. Obedience to fashion is pervading our Seventh-day Adventist churches and is doing more than any other power to separate our people from God. I have been shown that our church rules are very deficient. All exhibitions of pride in dress, which is forbidden in the word of God, should be sufficient reason for church discipline. If there is a continuance, in face of warnings and appeals and entreaties, to still follow the perverse will, it may be regarded as proof that the heart is in no way assimilated to Christ. Self, and only self, is the object of adoration, and one such professed Christian will lead many away from God" (Ellen G. White, *Testimonies for the Church*, vol. 4, p. 647).

Now we turn to the question of wearing jewelry or ornaments. The Bible teaches us that we should always be "proving what is acceptable unto the Lord" (Eph. 5:10). Our wedding rings and all other ornaments must be proved whether they are acceptable to the Lord, especially in this time of the end when nothing should get in our view of Jesus in the most holy place. Whatever we wear must reflect our love for God. Jesus tells us, "Thou shalt love the Lord thy God with all thy heart, and with all thy soul, and with all thy mind. This is the first and great commandment" (Matt. 22:37, 38). John reminds us that "whatsoever we ask, we receive of him, because we keep his commandments, and

Amusements and Secular Dressing

do those things that are pleasing in his sight" (1 John 3:22). Pleasing God extends to being careful lest we set a bad example and cause others to fall. Jesus warns us that, "Whoso shall offend one of these little ones which believe in me, it were better for him that a millstone were hanged about his neck, and that he were drowned in the depth of the sea" (Matt. 18:6).

If a remnant is moved by love for God and love for others, one will be sensitive to the slightest indication of God's will and will seek to please God rather than self. Such will hear the voice of God clearly say, "I will instruct thee and teach thee in the way which thou shalt go: I will guide thee with mine eye. Be ye not as the horse, or as the mule, which have no understanding: whose mouth must be held in with bit and bridle, lest they come near unto thee" (Ps. 32:8, 9).

Now of course one may ask, "What is wrong with my little armband or bracelet or ring or bangle?" That is a very sad question for any serious remnant to ask, but certainly one that needs an answer. The sadness lies in the implied attitude that reflects a legalistic desire to do only the things that are laid down as divine "do-it-or-else" laws. It would also imply a further question: "What can I get away with and remain a child of God?" The right question to ask is "How much can I do to please Jesus whom I love?" A remnant that understands the love Jesus offered to save us, the advocacy our Lord is offering on our behalf in the heavenly courts, will not risk displeasing the loving Lord. Certainly, a serious remnant will not look for loopholes in God's law or seek to comply with the minimum requirement of God's will.

But an answer to the supposed first question needs to be given. Through the prophet Isaiah God sent one of the most scathing denunciations of ornaments that can be found anywhere in the Bible. Nowhere do we find a more direct and unequivocal revelation of God's feelings toward the wearing of ornaments. In Isaiah 3:16 God does not generalize about ornaments—instead, He gives a long list of specific

Awakening the Remnant

articles that were being worn by the "daughters of Zion." Remember, God is the same yesterday, today, and forever, and if God was not pleased then, He certainly is not pleased today with the wearing of these things.

God said, "Moreover the LORD saith, Because the daughters of Zion are haughty, and walk with stretched forth necks and wanton eyes, walking and mincing as they go, and making a tinkling with their feet . . . In that day the Lord will take away the bravery of their tinkling ornaments about their feet, and their cauls . . . The chains, and the bracelets, and the mufflers . . . the ornaments of the legs, and the headbands, and the tablets, and the earrings, The rings, and nose jewels" (Isa. 3:16-21). In the next chapter, vwe read: "When the Lord shall have washed away the filth of the daughters of Zion . . . by the spirit of burning" (Isa. 4:4).

Here you notice that God refers to all these objects of adornment as "filth." He further describes most graphically the ones who survive the "washing away" of the ornaments: "In that day shall the branch of the LORD be beautiful and glorious, and the fruit of the earth shall be excellent and comely for them that are escaped of Israel. And it shall come to pass, that he that is left in Zion, and he that remaineth in Jerusalem, shall be called holy, even every one that is written among the living in Jerusalem" (Isa. 4:2, 3).

God uses that word "comely" to describe His saints, the church. "I have likened the daughter of Zion to a comely and delicate woman" (Jer. 6:2). As if to reinforce His assessment of the type of pride under consideration, God made the following observation: "The shew of their countenance doth witness against them; and they declare their sin as Sodom, they hide it not. Woe unto their soul! for they have rewarded evil unto themselves" (Isa. 3:9). No question is permitted to remain about the impropriety of outward adornment.

Amusements and Secular Dressing

Turning to the New Testament, the picture comes into even sharper focus. John, in the book of Revelation, describes the scarlet woman of sin (symbolizing the false church) as "decked with gold and precious stones and pearls, having a golden cup in her hand full of abominations and filthiness of her fornication" (Rev. 17:4). In contrast, the true church is depicted in Revelation 12:1 as a beautiful woman clothed with the glory of the sun. This woman represents the faithful saints in earth's history. Notice that the church of Christ wears no ornaments. These types of the true and the false religious systems also point up the lack of value that God places upon the use of artificial adornment.

Paul wrote, "In like manner also, that women adorn themselves in modest apparel, with shamefacedness and sobriety; not with broided hair, or gold, or pearls, or costly array; But (which becometh women professing godliness) with good works" (1 Tim. 2:9, 10).

One may still ask the question: what about the wedding ring? Again, it is a sad question, but one that needs an answer. We first encounter the use of a ring (not a wedding ring, but a mere ring) in Genesis 41:42 when Pharaoh took his off and put it on Joseph's hand. This occasion was not a wedding. The ring here was used as a symbol of power and authority. Even then, this symbolism was not a command from God, but devised by an idolatrous king. Many Egyptian customs, including the use of jewelry, were copied by the Israelites. In Exodus 32:3 and 4 we find Aaron making a golden calf from the ornaments of jewelry given to him by the Israelites.

We find in Exodus 33:5 God telling the Israelites to strip off the ornaments: "For the LORD had said unto Moses, Say unto the children of Israel, Ye are a stiffnecked people: I will come up into the midst of thee in a moment, and consume thee: therefore now put off thy ornaments from thee, that I may know what to do unto thee." What God demanded of the Israelites, He demands of us today. Indeed, the Israelites hearkened to the command. In verse 6 we read: "And the

Awakening the Remnant

children of Israel stripped themselves of their ornaments by the mount Horeb."

We have no Scripture where God ever told the Israelites they could put jewelry back on! If God said to take it off and gave no authorization to put it back on, then these ornaments of jewelry are forever to remain off the body of God's chosen people. One of the sins of King Saul was that he allowed the women to put back on ornaments (2 Sam. 1:24); and we all know Saul's fate.

In Jeremiah 4:30 the daughters of Israel decked themselves again with ornaments of gold, painted their faces, and made themselves beautiful (fair), but God said even with all this her lovers would despise her. Rings on the hands of a whore or harlot do not symbolize holiness or purity. These symbolize more the spirit of a witch, a woman who uses all available powers to seduce her victim to lust after her. Such fornication and adultery profanes the sacrifice of purity and holiness. (Read Ezekiel 16:10-15 and 23:40 for further study.)

Ellen White was not silent on the question of wedding rings. She wrote, "We need not wear the sign, for we are not untrue to our marriage vow, and the wearing of the ring would be no evidence that we were true. I feel deeply over this leavening process which seems to be going on among us, in the conformity to custom and fashion. Not one penny should be spent for a circlet of gold to testify that we are married. In countries where the custom is imperative, we have no burden to condemn those who have their marriage ring; let them wear it if they can do so conscientiously; but let not our missionaries feel that the wearing of the ring will increase their influence one jot or tittle. If they are Christians, it will be manifest in their Christlikeness of character, in their words, in their works, in the home, in association with others; it will be evinced by their patience and long-suffering and kindliness. They will manifest the spirit of the Master, they will pos-

Amusements and Secular Dressing

sess His beauty of character, His loveliness of disposition, His sympathetic heart" (*Testimonies to Ministers and Gospel Workers*, p. 180).

A sad aspect of wearing ornaments is the implication that these things are often not the problem but rather merely the symptom of a much more serious problem—the lack of full surrender to the Lordship of Jesus. Many wish to have Jesus as Savior but not as Lord, telling them how to live. Satan knows that once he has gained a foothold in a remnant with a small ornament or small wedding ring, souls can be pushed into other forms of indulgences that displease God. With one compromise that displeases God, the spiritual senses are clouded and the soul is led into all sorts of sins such as little lies, a little fornication, and eventual total backsliding. When the heart is yielded and God is made first in the life, no convert will allow a little band or ring or any other ornament to stand in the way of uniting with our loved God who is displeased by this outward adornment. When love of Christ is stronger than love of self, then nothing will stand in the way, least of all a small band or ring or any type of ornament.

To recognize the dangers of amusements, especially sports, which most of our institutions and leaders enjoy at the peril of souls, is not an attack on our church or its institutions. Satan would be pleased to let you believe that addressing sports is an attack on the church, as many pastors have been corrupted by this evil. This and similar dangers have been recognized in the past. For example, in 1985, the president of the North Pacific Union stated, "We are at a crossroads in the church as to whether we will go the way of what we classify as mainline, nominal Protestantism, or whether we will uphold the standards of Scripture and the Spirit of Prophecy" (*Adventist Review*, August 1, 1985, p. 14).

Sadly, some of our pastors have chosen the "mainline" route, and they brag from the pulpit about what sports club they support. One pastor stated: "Where sports is concerned, I am a great enthusiast of sports as a means of exercise or even enjoyment as a former run-

Awakening the Remnant

ner, and footballer etc." (July 14, 2009). What a sad "mainline" route some of our pastors have taken! Shall these pastors repent and lead the church to salvation, or will they pursue "vainglory" and cause others to perish with them? Will sanctified laymen awaken sleeping souls or will they, for fear of disfellowship from the church, enjoy sports and remain silent as souls perish? Saints, "every one of us shall give account of himself to God" (Rom. 14:12).

Chapter 3

Worshiping Like Other Churches

We are almost in the bosom of the great controversy that began in heaven, as, once again, the worship question is vividly brought into view. Seventh-day Adventists may view those who worship on Sunday as having no biblical basis for departing from Sabbath worship, but Satan knows that as long as we can pattern our Sabbath worship after Sunday worship, we are no different and we cannot truly claim to worship God.

Errors tolerated for a long time have gradually been transformed into a new reformation that seeks to discard our pillars and lead us to worship like other churches. The prophet Ellen White saw this determination by our church to pattern after other churches, and she wrote, "A new order of things has come into the ministry. There is a desire to pattern after other churches, and simplicity and humility are almost unknown. The young ministers seek to be original, and to introduce new ideas and new plans for labor. Some open revival meetings, and by this means call large numbers into the church. But when the excitement is over, where are the converted ones? Repentance and confession of sin are not seen. The sinner is entreated to believe in Christ and accept Him, without regard to his past life of sin and rebellion. The heart is not broken. There is no contrition of soul. The supposed

Awakening the Remnant

converted ones have not fallen upon the Rock, Christ Jesus" (*Selected Messages*, bk. 2, p. 18).

There is nowadays almost uncontrollable determination on the part of our leaders to have worship styles and inventions that keep the members excited and aroused in their senses. This, leaders think (deceived by the devil) will keep members in the church. Speaking directly against this, Ellen White wrote, "New and strange things will continually arise to lead God's people into false excitement, religious revivals, and curious developments; but our people should not be subjected to any tests of human invention that will create controversy in any line" (*Mind, Character, and Personality*, vol. 1, p. 42).

In Leviticus 10 we read about two leaders, Nadab and Abihu, who brought strange fire into the holy place. God was displeased and destroyed these self-appointed leaders. If our leaders feel at liberty to offer strange fire today, they will be met with God's disapproval. The prophet commented on the fate of Nadab and Abihu: "God has not changed. He is as particular and exact in His requirements now as He was in the days of Moses. But in the sanctuaries of worship in our day, with the songs of praise, the prayers, and the teaching from the pulpit, there is not merely strange fire, but positive defilement" (*S.D.A. Bible Commentary*, Vol. 1, p. 1111). The strange fires today come in different forms, but they are still strange fire if without approval from the Word of God.

The great controversy that began in heaven was about worship. The Bible recognizes only two kinds of worship: true worship and false worship. An attempt to marry true and false worship is known as "Babylon." Because God's faithful followers have always resisted drifting toward Babylon, throughout history there have been clashes between true and false worship. The Bible teaches that in the end times—our time today—there is to be a final conflict over worship.

Worshiping Like Other Churches

Sunday worship is being prepared through our acceptance of all sorts of styles and activities from Sunday worshippers.

Satan's rebellion against God is centered on worship—the desire to be like the Most High (Isa. 14:12-14). The first death in human history, the death of Abel at the hands of his brother Cain, was the result of a clash between true and false worship (Gen. 4). The contest between Elijah and the priests of Baal had to do with worship (1 Kings 18). Daniel and the three Hebrew men in Babylon were tested on the issue of worship (Dan. 3 and 6). In the days of Esther and Mordecai, the issue was worship (Esther 3-8). One of the temptations of Christ in the wilderness was over worship (Matt. 4:9-10). It is no wonder that the last conflict in human history is also over worship (Rev. 13 and 14).

God's people are in danger of being led by policies similar to those initiated by king Jeroboam. He ignored the blueprint for worship and "took counsel" and "made two calves of gold" and told the people "behold thy gods" (1 Kings 12:28). He certainly did not consult the scripture of Moses or the spirit of prophecy through the prophet Ahijah (1 Kings 11:29). Possibly he took surveys and opinion polls to see what the people wanted and how they preferred to worship. Possibly then the experts wrote a manual or some policy that he adopted and made two calves for worship. He then instituted a worship of convenience instead of obedience, when he said, "it is too much for you to go up to Jerusalem" (1 Kings 12:28), hence worship the two calves.

Supporters of modern worship styles that have crept into our church do not realize that they persuade the members that "it is too much to go to Jerusalem"—it is too much to ask members to put away their jewelry, it is too much to ask members to "bow down upon our knees before God when we offer our petitions to Him" in prayer (*Selected Messages*, bk. 2, p. 312). The Bible describes this worship of convenience as the sin of Jeroboam the son of Nebat, "wherewith he

Awakening the Remnant

made Israel to sin" (1 Kings 16:26). Ellen White warns in the *S.D.A. Bible Commentary* that "ministers of God have been guilty of the sin of disregarding a 'Thus saith the Lord.'. . . God will reward them according to their works. . . . Christ says of them as He said of the Jewish leaders, 'In vain they do worship me, teaching for doctrines the commandments of men'" (vol. 4, p. 1149).

In the old days, God lamented about the sin committed by His people: "For my people have committed two evils; they have forsaken me the fountain of living waters, and hewed them out cisterns, broken cisterns, that can hold no water. . . . And now what hast thou to do in the way of Egypt, to drink the waters of Sihor? or what hast thou to do in the way of Assyria, to drink the waters of the river?" (Jer. 2:13, 18).

Today, our church is in danger of worshiping other gods through accepting worship styles, broken cisterns, from other churches around us. Those who accept the worship styles devised by other churches cannot effectively proclaim the three angels' messages. If those churches represent "Babylon," and if it is true that "Babylon is fallen," how can we call upon our brothers and sisters in "Babylon" to "come out of her, my people" (Rev. 18:4), when we ourselves are now returning to "Babylon" to receive instruction from her to make our worship services relevant?

Some will argue that other churches also have some truth we can learn. Clearly this is not an option open to us. "If God has any new light to communicate, He will let His chosen and beloved understand it, without their going to have their minds enlightened by hearing those who are in darkness and error. . . . God is displeased with us when we go to listen to error, without being obliged to go. . . and the light around us become contaminated with the darkness" (Ellen G. White, *Early Writings*, p. 124).

Let us examine some of these worship styles, most likely copied from other churches, and see if they are or not broken cisterns. First,

Worshiping Like Other Churches

we examine a worship style of applause or clapping hands, which has now crept into our church and is practiced in most of our innovative or contemporary church services. Applause is defined in most English dictionaries as an act of approbation and praise publicly expressed by clapping the hands, stamping or tapping with the feet, or acclamation. Also defined as a demonstration of approval by clapping the hands together. The question here is whether this applause or clapping of hands is approved by the sure Word of God for use in worship services.

One of the key Bible passages often quoted to justify applause in the church is Psalm 47:1 and 2: "O clap your hands, all ye people; shout unto God with the voice of triumph. For the LORD most high is terrible; he is a great King over all the earth." Notice, however, that God alone is the recipient of the clapping of hands. The applause is not directed to any human being. Even then, the psalmist is referring to a future time when the Lord is coronated as "King over all the earth." The people clapping are a church already triumphant, as they shout "with the voice of triumph."

Ellen White wrote, "The work is soon to close. The members of the church militant who have proved faithful will become the church triumphant" (*Evangelism*, p. 707). It is to that future time when the now church militant becomes the church triumphant, when victory over the beast and the devil is fully gained, the Psalmist foresaw the remnants clapping their hands and shouting unto God with the voice of triumph, shouting with triumph for the Lord most high who then is a great King over all the earth made new.

Clapping of hands is attributed to a coronation of a king. When Joash was introduced as the legitimate heir to the throne those who were present clapped their hands and shouted, "God save the king!" (2 Kings 11:12). A religious usage of clapping hands is found in Psalms 47:1 where the psalmist invites all peoples to clap their hands because the Lord is being proclaimed as King over all the earth. In Psalms

Awakening the Remnant

98:8 the people (as in floods or multitudes) are exhorted to praise the Lord and the hills to clap their hands because the Lord is coming as King and Judge of the earth. There we see that even nature will rejoice before the Lord when He comes, at a future time, as King and Judge of the whole world.

Until Jesus' second return, the present king of this earth is Satan, and the psalmist is not referring to a present king but a future King. In Matthew 4:9 Satan said to Jesus, "All these things will I give thee, if thou wilt fall down and worship me." Satan could contemplate giving all earthly things to Jesus because he (Satan) was the king of the earthly kingdom. Jesus refused Satan's offer of this present kingdom. Even when the people wanted to make Jesus king, He did not take the offer. We are told in John 6:15 that Jesus knew that the people wanted him to become king. The people planned to come get Jesus and make him their king. So Jesus left and went into the hills alone. Referring directly to the king or prince of the present earth, Jesus said in John 14:30 "for the prince of this world cometh, and hath nothing in me." Jesus later explained in John 18:36 that "my kingdom is not of this world: if my kingdom were of this world, then would my servants fight, that I should not be delivered to the Jews: but now is my kingdom not from hence."

For saints who accept Jesus, His kingdom is within us (Luke 17:21), and we will inherit the kingdom prepared for us (Matt. 25:34). But that is not what the psalmist is referring to in the above text. The psalmist is not referring to clapping for a king now in this present earthly kingdom whose king is Satan, but rather to clap in the future kingdom whose King will be Jesus. To clap for Christ in triumph when He is coronated as King of all the earth, "every member of His church militant must manifest the same qualities, if He would join the church triumphant" (Ellen G. White, *Fundamentals of Christian Education*, p. 179). Moreover, a careful study of the Bible indicates that clap-

Worshiping Like Other Churches

ping or applause, as creeping into our churches today, was not part of the worship service in the Old and New Testaments. Rather, as in so many things, the practice came out of a desire to "pattern after other churches" (Ellen G. White, *Selected Messages*, bk. 2, p. 18).

We must not worship like them or inquire of their worship styles or their gods. "Take heed to thyself that thou be not snared by following them, after that they be destroyed from before thee; and that thou enquire not after their gods, saying, How did these nations serve their gods? even so will I do likewise. Thou shalt not do so unto the LORD thy God: for every abomination to the LORD, which he hateth, have they done unto their gods; for even their sons and their daughters they have burnt in the fire to their gods. What thing soever I command you, observe to do it: thou shalt not add thereto, nor diminish from it" (Deut. 12:30-32). This text applies to the fallen churches, and warns the remnant church not to worship like those churches.

Just as today, Ellen White saw applause as a social expression of joy, appreciation, or approval. But she never recommended it for our worship services. For example, on one occasion in the 1880s, Ellen White was invited to speak at the Temperance Reform Club of Haverhill, Massachusetts, in a city auditorium seating one thousand people. She wrote concerning this experience: "I was stopped several times with clapping of hands and stomping of feet" (*Review and Herald*, 1984, p. 46). While she witnessed the enthusiasm of this non-Adventist audience, she never endorsed clapping or stomping of feet as examples for Adventist worship services.

Instead of approving applause for worship services, Ellen White warned about its dangers. Referring to applause, she said Christians are "to relinquish all selfish delights, all unholy passions, all that love of applause which is the food of the world" (*The Southern Work*, p. 17). Talking of King Saul, Ellen White said, "His standard of right

Awakening the Remnant

and wrong was the low standard of popular applause" (*Patriarchs and Prophets*, p. 650).

Warning ministers who love applause, Ellen White wrote, "Some ministers of ability who are now preaching present truth, love approbation. Applause stimulates them, as the glass of wine does the inebriate. Place these ministers where they have a small congregation which promises no special excitement and which provokes no decided opposition, and they will lose their interest and zeal, and appear as languid in the work as the inebriate when he is deprived of his dram. These men will fail to make real, practical laborers until they learn to labor without the excitement of applause" (*Testimonies for the Church*, vol. 3, p. 185).

Looking at things not essential to the gospel, Ellen White wrote, "An appearance of wealth or position, expensive architecture or furnishings, are not essential to the advancement of the work of God; neither are achievements that win applause from men and administer to vanity. Worldly display, however imposing, is of no value with God" (*Testimonies for the Church*, vol. 7, p. 143).

Applause, Ellen White said, causes one to be "puffed up" (*Signs of the Times*, January 28, 1897). Moreover, she saw applause as "a snare" (*Special Testimonies for Ministers and Workers*, no. 4, p. 25), something that can injure a person (*Testimonies for the Church*, vol. 4, p. 376), and that which can even influence a person to leave the church for the world (*Review and Herald*, June 28, 1897).

Pointing to Jesus, Ellen White wrote, "Jesus did not seek the admiration or the applause of men. He commanded no army. He ruled no earthly kingdom. He did not court the favor of the wealthy and honored of the world. He did not claim a position among the leaders of the nation. He dwelt among the lowly. He set at nought the artificial distinctions of society. The aristocracy of birth, wealth, talent, learning, rank, He ignored" (*The Ministry of Healing*, p. 197).

Worshiping Like Other Churches

Since 1844, we live in the Day of Atonement. The prophet wrote, "We are in the great day of atonement, and the sacred work of Christ for the people of God that is going on at the present time in the heavenly sanctuary should be our constant study. We should teach our children what the typical Day of Atonement signified and that it was a special season of great humiliation and confession of sins before God. The antitypical day of atonement is to be of the same character. Everyone who teaches the truth by precept and example will give the trumpet a certain sound. You need ever to cultivate spirituality, because it is not natural for you to be heavenly-minded. The great work is before us of leading the people away from worldly customs and practices, up higher and higher, to spirituality, piety, and earnest work for God" (*Testimonies for the Church*, vol. 5, p. 520).

Of the typical Day of Atonement, the Bible records: "For whatsoever soul it be that shall not be afflicted in that same day, he shall be cut off from among his people" (Lev. 23:29). In this antitypical Day of Atonement, there is no shouting with a "voice of triumph." It is rather a special season of great humiliation and confession of sins before God, lest we be cut off from among His people when the High Priest completes the work in the most holy place while our sins remain with us. Jesus is in heaven ministering as High Priest, not as King of all the earth. When probation closes, Jesus will put away the priestly garments and will close Himself with kingly robes. Until then, we cannot clap for Jesus the King. If we clap and shout with triumph, instead of humiliation and confession in this antitypical Day of Atonement, a counterfeited "Jesus" is honored.

We now turn to yet another worship style that involves waving and lifting hands, which also has unfortunately crept into our church. The practice of the waving of hands during worship is increasing in our churches. This practice is often seen as a non-verbal way of showing appreciation or an assent to what is being preached or sang. Some-

Awakening the Remnant

times the uplifted hand is also used during prayers. Often, the book of Psalms is used as the main support. A careful study of the Bible reveals that hands were only lifted in prayer, and the waving and lifting hands in other times as developing today is unbiblical and must therefore be discouraged.

There are a number of Bible passages that speak about the raising of hands. The overwhelming evidence in Scripture, however, suggests that the practice was normally employed in prayer and supplication. For example, in Psalm 28:2 it says, "Hear the voice of my supplications, when I cry unto thee, when I lift up my hands toward thy holy oracle." This is an attitude of prayer. Lamentations 3:41 says, "Let us lift up our heart with our hands unto God in the heavens." Psalm 63:1-6 communicates joy, praise, thanksgiving, and longing for God in prayer, especially the tone of verse 4.

Other texts that address the raising of hands are all in the context of prayer: Psalm 119:48, 141:2, 143:1, 6, 7; 1 Kings 8:54; Nehemiah 8:6; and Lamentations 2:19, 3:40-43. It is quite clear from the relevant Bible texts that the "lifting of hands" was used during prayer. It was not used to show appreciation, approval, or as a form of non-verbal applause. It was a gesture showing a person's desire to walk in the ways of the Lord and this was only used in prayer.

Moreover, even in prayer, it is only holy hands that should be lifted: "lifting up holy hands, without wrath and doubting" (1 Tim. 2:8). The lifting of hands in prayer is figurative of a character void of moral defilement with the hands symbolizing holy deeds. God calls for leaders who will have a living connection with God to lift up their holy hands in supplication for the people they lead to be spared.

We now consider other activities like gestures. Two passages from *Selected Messages*, book 3, read as follows: "Bodily exercise profiteth little. Everything that is connected in any way with religious worship should be dignified, solemn, and impressive. God is not pleased when

Worshiping Like Other Churches

ministers professing to be Christ's representatives so misrepresent Christ as to throw the body into acting attitudes, making undignified and coarse gestures, unrefined, coarse gesticulations. All this amuses, and will excite the curiosity of those who wish to see strange, odd, and exciting things, but these things will not elevate the minds and hearts of those who witness them."

"The very same may be said of singing. You assume undignified attitudes. You put in all the power and volume of the voice you can. You drown the finer strains and notes of voices more musical than your own. This bodily exercise and the harsh, loud voice makes no melody to those who hear on earth and those who listen in heaven. This singing is defective and not acceptable to God as perfect, softened, sweet strains of music. There are no such exhibitions among the angels as I have sometimes seen in our meetings. Such harsh notes and gesticulations are not exhibited among the angel choir. Their singing does not grate upon the ear. It is soft and melodious and comes without this great effort I have witnessed. It is not forced and strained, requiring physical exercise" (p. 333).

We now turn to what some regard as a forbidden subject, the question of use of drums in our worship services. The Bible is not opposed to the use of musical instruments. Ellen White encouraged the tasteful use of musical instruments. However, she was emphatic that it is better never to have the worship of God blended with music where the musical instruments create "a bedlam of noise" that shocks the senses and perverts the worship. "The Holy Spirit never reveals in such methods, in such a bedlam of noise" (*Selected Messages*, bk. 2, p. 36). She stressed that music suited to the stage was foreign to the worship context. Forced or strained vocal deliveries that emphasize loudness, along with undignified, unrefined gestures and "acting attitudes," are out of keeping with the worship atmosphere of heaven. The "softer," "finer," "sweeter," "more silvery strains" are "more like angel music,"

Awakening the Remnant

whereas opposite attributes tend to be driven by self-centered "love of praise" (*Selected Messages*, bk. 3, p. 335).

The Bible clearly does not sanction drums in worship. God never gave drums for use in the sanctuary worship. The Lord specified three types of instruments to be used by the Levites in the sanctuary: harp, lyre, and cymbals (1 Chron. 25:1). In this list, the drum is not mentioned. Of the three instruments mentioned, the harp and lyre were, essentially, the same type of stringed instrument. They were both harps. One (the harp) played the higher register while the other (the lyre) played the lower range. The only percussive instrument listed is cymbals, an instrument that was apparently used to mark the pauses or intermissions. The same three musical instruments are mentioned in 1 Chronicles 25:6, with added instruction that the chosen musicians were to be under the instruction of their fathers (men of music, and most importantly, spiritual excellence). In 2 Chronicles 29:25, during the time of Hezekiah, it is made very clear that the instruction regarding music, musical instruments, and musicians originated with God Himself.

Though drums were apparently not employed in the sanctuary service, they were used in festivals and celebrations outside of the sanctuary. Here are some relevant texts: Genesis 31:27; 1 Samuel 10:5-6; Job 17:6, 21:11-14; Psalm 81:2; Isaiah 24:8; Jeremiah 31:4; Ezekiel 28:13.

There are also instances in the Bible where drums were associated with disobedience. In Isaiah 5:11-13 drums are used in disobedience in Israel. In 1 Chronicles 13:7-10 David disobeyed God's commandment about how the ark was to be transported. Most people ignorantly use this text to support drums, because of the wording that David danced in the Lord. Clearly, David had simply disobeyed God, and the Bible simply records facts of what David claimed to do, dance in the Lord.

Worshiping Like Other Churches

When he later repented, he did the right thing. But this time, drums (timbrels) were not included (1 Chron. 15:12-24).

Drums were also associated with battle. In Exodus 15:1-5, 20-21, drums were used in connection with the victory over the Egyptians at the Red Sea. In Judges 11:34, Jephthah's daughter met her father "with timbrels and with dances." The celebration was in response to the victory in the battle over the Ammonites. In 1 Samuel 18:6 and 7 drums were used in celebration by the women after David killed Goliath. In Isaiah 30:31-33 drums were used in celebration over the Lord's victory over the Assyrians. In Psalm 149 drums were used in celebration of God's victory over all his enemies.

In Psalm 150 drums are used, but for some, verse 1 presents a problem because it speaks of praising God "in His sanctuary." However, Psalm 150 is the final great finale to the hallelujah series of psalms that begin with Psalm 146. Psalm 150 concludes this series with a final call for everything (whether on earth or in heaven) that has breath to join in the praise anthem of God. Verse 1 is simply an invitation to those in heaven (the heavenly sanctuary) to worship God in "the firmament of His power" (see *S.D.A. Bible Commentary*, vol. 3, p. 941, revised edition). The text reads: "Praise God in his sanctuary [which is in] . . . the firmament of his power."

Note that drums associated with battle emphasize the celebration that takes place when God granted victory. But some will say, we must use drums and dancing in the church to celebrate the victories God has given us in our spiritual battles over sin. The question is: did the Israelites win spiritual battles over sin in their lives? How come the Bible does not give a record of that? It is interesting that there is no reference to drums (timbrel) being used in the New Testament. Historical records showed that drumming and dancing were banned because of their association with common and profane things. And now some of our sister Adventist churches use drums that were never sanctioned by

Awakening the Remnant

the God we worship. Just because our local conferences make policies that allow for these contemporary drum uses in worship, does it make it right with God? Can we point at conference policy to truly enjoin that which God disjoined? Must we be silent about this trend of unbiblical sanction of drums and worship styles?

We now turn to dancing in our worship service. After a careful study of the Bible, one can conclude that (1) Scripture and history indicate that dancing was never part of divine worship in the temple, synagogue, or early church, (2) of the 28 references to dance or dancing in the Old Testament, only four can be considered to refer to religious dancing (Ps. 149:3, 150:4; 2 Sam. 6:14-16), but none of these relate to worship in God's house, and two of them may not actually refer to dancing at all, (3) social dancing in Bible times was done mostly in conjunction with the celebration of religious events, especially the annual festivals, and performed outside the temple by women, children, or men, as separate groups, and not as male-female couples; and (4) the Levitical choir was to be accompanied only by stringed instruments, the harp and the lyre (1 Chron. 16:42; 2 Chron. 5:12-14); percussion instruments like drums and tambourines, which were commonly used for making dance music, were clearly omitted.

David, who is regarded by many as the primary example of religious dancing in the Bible, never instructed the Levites regarding when and how to dance in the temple. Had David believed that dancing should be a component of divine worship, no doubt he would have given instructions regarding it to the Levite musicians he chose for the ministry of music at the temple. Also, David is the founder of the music ministry at the temple. He gave clear instruction to the 4,000 Levite musicians regarding when to sing and what instruments to use to accompany their choir (1 Chron. 23:5, 25-31). His omission of dancing in divine worship can hardly be an oversight. Rather, it tells us that David distinguished between the sacred music performed

Worshiping Like Other Churches

in God's house and the secular music played outside the temple for entertainment.

Often, dancing, drumming, and shouting are characteristics of pagan worship. The Bible records examples of such practices in Exodus 32 (apostasy that was led by Aaron) and 1 Kings 18 (in connection with the Baal worshippers on Mount Carmel). Ellen White also wrote that shortly before probation closes for the world, drumming and dancing will be introduced into the worship services of the church. Though proponents will claim that such expressions are evidence of the Spirit's leading, according to Ellen White, no encouragement should be given it—for it is Satan's counterfeit to deceive. She made this prophecy in connection with a similar event that took place at a Muncie, Indiana, camp meeting in 1900 (*Selected Messages*, bk. 2, pp. 36, 37).

Faithful leaders in our Seventh-day Adventist church must discourage their members from use of applause, waving of hands, drumming, and dancing in the church. These practices in the contemporary worship services are a twenty-first century Jeroboam worship experience that only brings a curse. Ellen White calls upon us to take a decided stand against this "frivolity" and "nonsense" that can only lead to "perdition" (*The Adventist Home*, pp. 407, 408).

We now turn to the question of proper prayer posture in our worship service. This is sadly painful, but must be addressed. The church manual, which has almost turned into a creed for some ministers, addressing first the pastoral prayer, states: "It is customary to kneel, facing the congregation, and the congregation in turn should face the rostrum and, as far as practicable, kneel" and then for other prayer, "congregation standing or seated" (*Church Manual*, 2005 version, pp. 95,96). Just as King Jeroboam failed to consult the prophet of God, some ministers fail to consult the church prophet, who, addressing all worship prayer, states: "Both in public and in private worship it is

Awakening the Remnant

our privilege to bow on our knees before God when we offer our petitions to Him. Jesus, our example, 'kneeled down, and prayed.' Luke 22:41. Of his disciples it is recorded that they, too, 'kneeled down, and prayed.' Acts 9:40. Paul declared, 'I bow my knees unto the Father of our Lord Jesus Christ.' Ephesians 3:14. In confessing before God the sins of Israel, Ezra knelt. See Ezra 9:5. Daniel 'kneeled upon his knees three times a day, and prayed, and gave thanks before his God.' Daniel 6:10" (*Prophets and Kings*, p. 48). With a conflict between the church manual guide and the inspired prophetic counsel in the Spirit of Prophecy, on prayer posture, true remnants must decidedly follow God in the Sprit of Prophecy.

Jesus shows up in our worship every Sabbath; we behold Him by faith; in adoration, the respectful congregation stands for Jesus. Must we follow the crowd in offering a standing ovation to Jesus when the Word of God clearly states "that at the name of Jesus every knee should bow" (Phil. 2:10)? As if in mockery, some of our churches customarily sing the introit to Jesus—"O come, let us worship and bow down: let us kneel before the LORD our maker" (Ps. 95:6)—and then they stand to worship in prayer! Jesus Himself "kneeled down, and prayed" (Luke 22:41). Elijah "cast himself down upon the earth, and put his face between his knees" to plead for rain (1 Kings 18:42). Should we rise on our feet to plead for the latter rain?

Ellen White speaks directly to us in *Selected Messages*, book 2: "We are living in perilous times. Seventh-day Adventists are professedly the commandment-keeping people of God; but they are losing their devotional spirit. This spirit of reverence for God teaches men how to approach their Maker—with sacredness and awe through faith, not in themselves, but in a Mediator. Thus man is kept fast, under whatever circumstances he is placed. Man must come on bended knee, as a subject of grace, a suppliant at the footstool of mercy" (p. 314). In the same book, page 312, she states: "Both in public and private wor-

Worshiping Like Other Churches

ship it is our duty to bow down upon our knees before God when we offer our petitions to Him. This act shows our dependence upon God." Note that to the prophet, kneeling in worship is our duty, yet church policies portray this as merely customary. Must we exchange biblical and Spirit of Prophecy teaching on prayer posture for church policy that teaches that we must stand in all worship prayer sessions and only kneel in pastoral prayer?

Ellen White repeated the emphasis on kneeling in prayer in the book *Gods Amazing Grace*, page 91: "Both in public and in private worship, it is our duty to bow upon our knees before God when we offer our petitions to Him. Jesus, our example, 'kneeled down, and prayed.' And of His disciples it is recorded that they, too, 'kneeled down, and prayed.' Stephen 'kneeled.' Paul declared: 'I bow my knees unto the Father of our Lord Jesus Christ' (Ephesians 3:14). In confessing before God the sins of Israel, Ezra knelt. Daniel 'kneeled upon his knees three times a day, and prayed, and gave thanks before his God' (Daniel 6:10). And the invitation of the psalmist is: 'O come, let us worship and bow down: let us kneel before the Lord our Maker' (Psalm 95:6)."

Of course, outside worship dictates that "you cannot always be on your knees in prayer, but your silent petitions may constantly ascend to God for strength and guidance" (*In Heavenly Places*, p. 86). As you go along your daily duties during the week—when working for income, when in the fields tendering the plants, when driving to work, when talking to your employer—you should always "pray without ceasing" (1 Thess. 5:17). We have only examined worship prayer posture above in the context of the worship service.

In these last days, there are two classes of worshipers, the careful and the careless. In the book *Early Writings*, Ellen White wrote: "I saw a throne, and on it sat the Father and the Son. . . . I saw two companies, one bowed down before the throne, deeply interested, while

Awakening the Remnant

the other stood uninterested and careless. Those who were bowed before the throne would offer up their prayers and look to Jesus; then He would look to His Father, and appear to be pleading with Him. A light would come from the Father to the Son and from the Son to the praying company. Then I saw an exceeding bright light come from the Father to the Son, and from the Son it waved over the people before the throne. But few would receive this great light. Many came out from under it and immediately resisted it; others were careless and did not cherish the light, and it moved off from them. Some cherished it, and went and bowed down with the little praying company. This company all received the light and rejoiced in it, and their countenances shone with its glory.

"I saw the Father rise from the throne, and in a flaming chariot go into the holy of holies within the veil, and sit down. Then Jesus rose up from the throne, and the most of those who were bowed down arose with Him. I did not see one ray of light pass from Jesus to the careless multitude after He arose, and they were left in perfect darkness. Those who arose when Jesus did, kept their eyes fixed on Him as He left the throne and led them out a little way. . . . Those who rose up with Jesus would send up their faith to Him in the holiest, and pray, 'My Father, give us Thy Spirit.' Then Jesus would breathe upon them the Holy Ghost. In that breath was light, power, and much love, joy, and peace.

"I turned to look at the company who were still bowed before the throne; they did not know that Jesus had left it. Satan appeared to be by the throne, trying to carry on the work of God. I saw them look up to the throne, and pray, 'Father, give us Thy Spirit.' Satan would then breathe upon them an unholy influence; in it there was light and much power, but no sweet love, joy, and peace. Satan's object was to keep them deceived and to draw back and deceive God's children" (pp. 54-56).

Worshiping Like Other Churches

The small careful worshippers ask for the Spirit of Jesus, and are answered by Jesus, for they worship with their eyes fixed on Jesus and keep their garments spotless. The multitude of careless worshippers also ask for the Spirit of Jesus, but Satan answers their prayers, for they worship like the rest of the fallen churches worship. Those who despise prophesyings (1 Thess. 5:20) and reject the Spirit of Prophesy (Rev. 12:17, 19:10) are the same who reject the light of Jesus and worship like others churches with their prayers for Jesus' Spirit answered by Satan.

We now consider other worship styles. These too will creep into the church if it has not already happened. There is a growing determination amongst ministers to make the Word of God relevant to young people and modern children. Worship services are gradually being transformed to include all sorts of inventions such as drama, mime, raps, videos, shadow plays, sketch, interactive story, and mini sermon presented by a child. The negative effect of these gimmicks is often ignored.

There is also the age movement that is determined to have separate divine worship services for different ages, with children having sermons relevant to them. All to the mind that lacks the guidance of the Holy Spirit seems all right. The Elijah message in Malachi 4:5 and 6 is irrelevant to these age ministers. The Word of God tells us what Elijah will do: "And he shall turn the heart of the fathers to the children, and the heart of the children to their fathers, lest I come and smite the earth with a curse." Contrary to the end-time work of Elijah, these age ministers pursue worship styles that are bound to produce opposite effects.

As a remnant church, we have failed to learn lessons from the Old Testament. In Exodus 24:7 we read the pledge of the people: "All that the LORD hath said we will do, and be obedient." Then Moses went to meet God, leaving the people with Aaron in charge. In Exodus 32:1-

Awakening the Remnant

6, because Moses delayed to return, the people said to the minister, Aaron, "Up, make us gods, which shall go before us" for we do not know what has become of Moses. The temporarily corrupted minister, Aaron, after making idol gods, "made proclamation, and said, To morrow is a feast to the LORD." What a mockery to God! The next day, in their worship of idol gods, they "offered burnt offerings, and brought peace offerings; and the people sat down to eat and to drink, and rose up to play." We know that Aaron repented of his sin.

The remnant church today, because of the perceived delay of the return of Jesus, by our indifference or otherwise, has asked our compromised ministers to make us gods like the ones worshipped by the other churches, to lighten our journey to heaven. Our ministers, corrupted with scholarly theological "wine of Babylon," which has gradually crept into our institutions, have made new theology idols that seek to make worship celebratory to suit feelings of modern Christianity, and they have proclaimed "a feast to the Lord." These new theology ideas are now almost entrenched in all aspects of our positions. This is why strange doctrines appear in our official church publications, and we hardly notice. This is why our Sabbath School Lesson Quarterlies have been watered down, and we hardly notice. This is why there are drums in the church; if they are not yet in your church, wait, they are coming! This is why there is dancing and clapping in the church, characteristic of when Israel "rose up to play," which is officiated upon by modern Aaron ministers.

Notice the language between God and Moses about whose people they were that worshipped idol gods. First, God calls the people Moses' people: "And the LORD said unto Moses, Go, get thee down; for thy people, which thou broughtest out of the land of Egypt, have corrupted themselves" (Ex. 32:7). Second, Moses calls the people God's people: "And Moses besought the LORD his God, and said, LORD, why doth thy wrath wax hot against thy people, which thou

Worshiping Like Other Churches

hast brought forth out of the land of Egypt with great power, and with a mighty hand?" (verse 11). God mercifully gave Moses a taste of intercessory work.

God calls faithful ministers today to intercede so that as a church we repent of our idolatry. The prophet Joel echoes this call: "Let the priests, the ministers of the LORD, weep between the porch and the altar, and let them say, Spare thy people, O LORD, and give not thine heritage to reproach, that the heathen should rule over them: wherefore should they say among the people, Where is their God?" (Joel 2:17). Will you, as a faithful minister, like Moses, ask your other erring ministers, the Aaron-types, this question, "What did this people unto thee, that thou has brought so great a sin upon them?" (Ex. 32:21).

Faithful ministers should no longer be silent about these modern idols in our worship—peradventure people will turn to God and corrupt ministers may also repent, as did Aaron. Moses bravely stood at the gate of the camp and called out: "Who is on the LORD's side?" (Ex. 32:26) before commanding a slaughter of the wicked (verse 27): "And the children of Levi did according to the word of Moses: and there fell of the people that day about three thousand men" (verse 28).

In contrast, after the truth had been rejected—Jesus was rejected and crucified—the apostle Peter conducted a revival, used the Word of God as a sword, and called people to repent of their sin of crucifying Jesus. The results: "Then they that gladly received his word were baptized: and the same day there were added unto them about three thousand souls" (Acts 2:41). Let God's faithful ministers lift up the Word of God and preach to the people: repent, repent, and repent!

The Spirit of Prophecy has truth we should not ignore. In *The Great Controversy* Ellen White wrote, "What was the origin of the great apostasy? How did the church first depart from the simplicity of the gospel?—By conforming to the practices of paganism, to facilitate the acceptance of Christianity by the heathen. The apostle Paul declared, even in his day, 'The mystery of iniquity doth already work.' [2 Thessalonians 2:7.] During the lives of the apostles the church remained comparatively pure. 'But toward the latter end of the second century most of the churches assumed a new form, the first simplicity disappeared; and insensibly, as the old disciples retired to their graves, their children, along with new converts ... came forward and new-modeled the cause.' [Robinson, in History of Baptism.] To secure converts, the exalted standard of the Christian faith was lowered, and as the result 'a pagan flood, flowing into the church, carried with it its customs, practices, and idols.' [Gavazzi's Lectures, p. 290.] As the Christian religion secured the favor and support of secular rulers, it was nominally accepted by multitudes; but while in appearance Christians, many 'remained in substance pagans, especially worshiping in secret their idols.' [Gavazzi's Lectures, p. 290.]" (p. 384).

Today, ministers are interested only in numbers; the unconverted are baptized, sin is not rebuked in church lest people leave, and the result is all sorts of paganism creeping into the church!

In these last days of earth's history, with the lines between truth and error confusing, we must worship God "in spirit and in truth" (John 4:23). If we try any other terms of worship, or copy worship styles from the fallen churches in order to arouse excitement in the worship experience, we risk drinking from broken cisterns. Ours is not a mission to join worship styles of the fallen churches, but to call our brothers and sisters in those churches to "come out of her, my people" (Rev. 18:4). Leave alone these strange worship styles!

Those who despise Ellen White's counsel are taking the "First Step Toward Apostasy.—One thing is certain: Those Seventh-day Adventists who take their stand under Satan's banner will first give up their faith in the warnings and reproofs contained in the testimonies of God's Spirit. If you lose confidence in the *Testimonies* you will drift

Worshiping Like Other Churches

away from Bible truth" (Ellen G. White, *The Publishing Ministry*, p. 360).

While many leaders would be horrified to discover that members looked upon them as any kind of infallible deciders of truth, some of our members regard our leaders as such! Satan, having implanted that regard in the minds of members, "spares no pains to corrupt men in responsible positions and to persuade them to be unfaithful to their several trusts" (Ellen G. White, *Testimonies for the Church*, vol. 4, p. 210).

In the name of unity, corrupted leaders then pass false worship to members. "Christ calls for unity. But He does not call for us to unify on wrong practices. The God of heaven draws a sharp contrast between pure, elevating, ennobling truth and false, misleading doctrines. He calls sin and impenitence by the right name. He does not gloss over wrongdoing with a coat of untempered mortar. I urge our brethren to unify upon a true, scriptural basis" (Ellen G. White, *Selected Messages*, bk. 1, p. 175). Awaken ye saints!

Chapter 4

Diet Reform is Not an Option

The enemy of souls, having begun the great controversy in heaven, sought his war on the remnants when he first tempted man through appetite. By indulging man into appetite, Satan hopes to be worshiped. As Seventh-day Adventists we may deny direct devil worship, but Satan knows that as long as we continue perverting our appetite with diseased flesh of this world while we claim to worship God, he will still be indirectly worshiped. The simple truth is this: when God freed the Israelites from Egypt, He changed their diet from meat to manna. Those who disobeyed perished in the wilderness, and they worshipped idols. When the Israelites were captive in Babylon, they had to change their diet from meat to pulse; those who disobeyed all worshipped Nebuchadnezzar's statute. Clearly, worshiping the devil follows indulgence in diet. We are in danger of perishing in this world and worshiping the beast of Revelation 13 unless we change our diet from animal based to plant based.

Our neglect of health reform is also a neglect of preaching an effective three angels' message of Revelation 14. Our time is that of a call from God in Isaiah 60:1 "Arise, shine; for thy light is come, and the glory of the LORD is risen upon thee." With an undiluted health reform message, we must shine and lighten the world with God's glo-

Awakening the Remnant

ry of healing. We are also living in the time of the fourth angel of Revelation 18:1 who gives us power to spread the three angels' message: "And after these things I saw another angel come down from heaven, having great power; and the earth was lightened with his glory."

Using the health reform as a wedge, we are to be the voice of the fourth angel and as in Revelation 18:4 be heard: "And I heard another voice from heaven, saying, Come out of her, my people, that ye be not partakers of her sins, and that ye receive not of her plagues." If we who are meant to warn others to reform continue with our bad diets, we will cause our bodies to be diseased, making a fertile ground for the "plagues" meant for the rebellious wicked.

One of the most overlooked branches of the gospel is the one the Spirit of Prophecy calls the right arm of the gospel. The health and wellness of the people of God should be as distinct as the complete system of truth that God in His infinite wisdom has given the Seventh-day Adventist Church. We are told: "When properly conducted, the health work is an entering wedge, making a way for other truths to reach the heart. When the third angel's message is received in its fullness, health reform will be given its place in the councils of the conference, in the work of the church, in the home, at the table, and in all the household arrangements. Then the right arm will serve and protect the body" (*Testimonies for the Church*, vol. 6, p. 327).

As a remnant, God desires that we return to our previous state before sin, and so He has given us the methods to accomplish that, and one method or avenue is through diet reform. Some do not see the connection, but it is vitally connected, as we are told: "In order to render to God perfect service, you must have clear conceptions of His requirements. You should use the most simple food, prepared in the most simple manner, that the fine nerves of the brain be not weakened, benumbed, or paralyzed, making it impossible for you to discern sacred things, and to value the atonement, the cleansing blood of Christ,

Diet Reform is Not an Option

as of priceless worth" (Ellen G. White, *Testimonies for the Church*, vol. 2, p. 46).

For us as the remnants, we should ever remember that we are living in the antitypical Day of Atonement, and because we are, we have to go to the Bible and get an accurate view that can guide us on how we should conduct ourselves on the Day of Atonement. It was clear on that day because of the magnitude of the outcome whether you remained with God's chosen people (representative of being saved) or whether you were banished from the camp (representative of being lost). The Israelites made sure that every sin had been confessed and that the blood was on the curtain before the Day of Atonement. Also, they fasted on that day as well as the days leading up to it to bring the body into subjection so as not to commit sin. It should be the same for us today, though we cannot fast for a lifetime, our diets should reflect a type of fast, thus going back to eating simple foods prepared in a most simple way so as not to injure the body, benumb the brain, and spiritually blind us to the requirements of the Creator.

But above all, we must know how the devil uses diet to cause us to fall and worship him. Every thing the devil does is about worship. It is through perverted appetites that the devil plans to have Sabbath-keepers, the remnants, worship him. Ellen White was shown a vision where Satan planned to ensnare us with appetite. The prophet wrote:

"But our principal concern is to silence this sect of Sabbath keepers. We must excite popular indignation against them. . . . 'But before proceeding to these extreme measures, we must exert all our wisdom and subtlety do deceive and ensnare those who honor the true Sabbath. We can separate many from Christ by worldliness, lust, and pride. They may think themselves safe because they believe the truth, but indulgence of appetite or the lower passions, which will confuse judgment and destroy discrimination, will cause their fall'" (*Testimonies to Ministers and Gospel Workers*, p. 473).

Awakening the Remnant

If this is the devil's plan, why must we succumb to it after we are clearly warned? If we truly have an appetite problem, why, like any other habit, must we not take it to the Lord in prayer?

Some are so ensnared by appetite that they do not even realize that we are in a health crisis. The world has no health hope without Seventh-day Adventists putting the health message out there. We have forgotten who we are and have lost our identity. We are called of God to bring to people the eternal gospel twined with a message of healing. Why allow God to bring in new people to do the work that we have refused to do?

Since the great controversy began in heaven, Satan has always sought to use appetite to control the human mind and finally to have all men worship him. Even for health benefits, men ought to wake up to the dangers of flesh eating. Incredibly, the large block of flesh-eating Seventh-day Adventists seems the hardest to impress. In the face of pages and books of divine warnings, admonitions and pleas, thousands of laymen and ministers continue to eat the flesh of animals. No wonder few know that Satan is ensnaring us with perversion of appetite.

If only for the sake of good health, many should revisit their diet. Even then, many do not remember that God's promise on health is conditional upon us obeying Him. In Exodus 15:26 we read: "And said, If thou wilt diligently hearken to the voice of the LORD thy God, and wilt do that which is right in his sight, and wilt give ear to his commandments, and keep all his statutes, I will put none of these diseases upon thee, which I have brought upon the Egyptians: for I am the LORD that healeth thee."

It is sad that the world is disobedient, and we who should know better are on the same train with the devil driving the train. We are all crippled in health yet we claim our body temples are destined for heaven. The devil laughs as he scorns, which heaven? For the devil

Diet Reform is Not an Option

knows that, if any man defile the body temple by the effects of his perverted appetite, "him shall God destroy" (1 Cor. 3:17).

We often forget that the statutes on health were given for a perpetual time: "It shall be a perpetual statute for your generations throughout all your dwellings, that ye eat neither fat nor blood" (Leviticus 3:17). We see this repeated to Christians in Acts 15:29: "That ye abstain from meats offered to idols, and from blood, and from things strangled, and from fornication: from which if ye keep yourselves, ye shall do well. Fare ye well." It is also for our own good that God gave us health laws. If we obey these, He will "put none of these diseases upon" us.

The more we have disobeyed, sin has increased in the world and so have diseases in both man and animals. As a result of sin, "the whole creation groaneth" (Rom. 8:22), "even we ourselves groan within ourselves" (verse 23), and "the Spirit itself maketh intercession for us with groanings" (verse 26). What we must do is instructed to us in prophecy, both in the Bible and in the Spirit of Prophecy. We often know what to do, but because we are controlled by appetite, we ignore counsel.

In the beginning, God in His infinite wisdom never appointed to man flesh, but plants for food. Man was to be vegan, eating no flesh. This original plan for man's food was before sin and was a perfect plan. The all-wise God knew our needs, and He determined what food Adam must have. We read in Genesis 1:29: "Behold," God said, "I have given you every herb bearing seed . . . and every tree, in the which is the fruit of a tree yielding seed; to you it shall be for meat."

After sin, upon leaving Eden to gain his livelihood by tilling the earth under the curse of sin, man received permission to eat also "the herb of the field," which was still a plant diet. We then find that grains, fruits, nuts, and vegetables constituted the diet chosen for us by our kind and wise Creator. The original man's plant diet, prepared in as simple and natural a manner as possible, is the most healthful and

Awakening the Remnant

nourishing. This imparts strength, a power of endurance, and vigor of intellect that are not afforded by a more complex and stimulating diet. It is to this simple diet God wants us to return.

It is after the Flood that we find flesh allowed to man for food. God then gave statutes concerning "the beast that may be eaten and the beast that may not be eaten" (Lev. 11:47). Of creatures that are on land, Leviticus 11:3 tells us to eat those that "parteth the hoof . . . and cheweth the cud." From this we know we can eat cows and sheep. We know we cannot eat pigs. We know that lions and tigers are carnivorous and not to be eaten. Of creatures in the water, Leviticus 11:9 tells us to eat those that have "fins and scales." The same instruction is given in Deuteronomy 14:9. We know that shellfish are not to be eaten. Of creatures of the air, we have clean and unclean birds. We know from Leviticus 11:13 and Deuteronomy 14:13 that birds of prey are not to be eaten.

Even though God allowed man to eat flesh, it was never His original plan. Before sin, man was to eat the best food, which composed of only a plant-based diet. We read in Numbers 11 that God gave the Israelites a plant diet called manna, which was purely a vegan diet. The prophet Ellen White tells us why God gave the Israelites manna: "The state of the mind has largely to do with the health of the body, and especially with the health of the digestive organs. As a general thing, the Lord did not provide His people with flesh meat in the desert, because He knew that the use of this diet would create disease and insubordination. In order to modify the disposition, and bring the higher powers of the mind into active exercise, He removed from them the flesh of dead animals. He gave them angel's food, manna from heaven" (*S.D.A. Bible Commentary*, vol. 1, p. 1112).

One would think that the Israelites appreciated this "angel's food, manna from heaven." However, Numbers 11:6 records their attitude. They complained that they had "nothing at all, beside this manna" to

Diet Reform is Not an Option

eat. They demanded flesh meat they had eaten in Egypt. Moses grew perplexed, for the people become hostile for the want of flesh to eat, rejecting the "angel's food, manna from heaven." They disobeyed. God gave positive evidence that He rules in the heavens, and rebellion was punished with death. Only two of those who as adults left Egypt saw the Promised Land (Num. 26:65). They wandered, and the wanderings were extended until the rest were buried in the wilderness.

Today, Satan is using the same tactics to introduce the same evils, and his efforts are followed by the same results that in the days of Israel laid so many in their graves.

The rest of the history of the Israelites is recorded in the Bible as a life of ups and downs, with mixed diets of flesh and plants. Fortunately, God in His mercy never gave up on these rebellious people. God then tells the Israelites, "Thou shalt not eat any abominable thing" (Deut. 14:3).

The same God speaks through Paul to explain the principle that should govern our diet, whether be of plants or flesh: the body temple principle. We read in 1 Corinthians 3:16 and 17, "Know ye not that ye are the temple of God, and that the Spirit of God dwelleth in you? If any man defile the temple of God, him shall God destroy; for the temple of God is holy, which temple ye are." And the parallel in the heavenly city is given in Revelation 21:27: "And there shall in no wise enter into it any thing that defileth, neither whatsoever worketh abomination, or maketh a lie: but they which are written in the Lamb's book of life." Whatever we eat then should not disease or defile the body temple, lest the Holy Spirit grieve and leave. Let us examine some of the defiling examples.

Fat and blood, even in clean creatures, is not to be eaten. It says in Leviticus 3:17, "It shall be a perpetual statute for your generations throughout all your dwellings, that ye eat neither fat nor blood." We see this repeated to Christians in Acts 15:29: "That ye abstain from meats offered to idols, and from blood, and from things strangled, and from fornication: from which if ye keep yourselves, ye shall do well. Fare ye well." Today people go for Kosher meats to avoid blood. Most people find this blunt without taste, for lack of blood and/or fat. Most remnants do not even seek out kosher meats; they eat whatever is in the market. It is very sad that God's people are reduced to this animal-like level!

Even clean creatures that have been torn by beast are not to be eaten. It says in Exodus 22:31, "And ye shall be holy men unto me: neither shall ye eat any flesh that is torn of beasts in the field; ye shall cast it to the dogs." Beasts of prey, such as lions, tend to attack weak and sick animals who are defenseless or cannot escape faster. God does not want us to eat of these weak and sick animals.

Creatures that "dieth of itself" are not to be eaten (Deut. 14:21). In most cases, it is weak and sick or diseased animals that tend to die; these are not to be eaten. The same principle applies to sick diseased animals that are slaughtered to prevent them from dying. Many animals slaughtered in the markets are downer animals, with no difference with what is prohibited, and yet even the remnants feed on these carcasses. It must be a terrible ordeal for our Creator, who first appointed a plant diet for man, to watch His peculiar people eat abominably!

Abominable meats, whether of clean or unclean creatures, are not to be eaten. We are told in Deuteronomy 14:3, "Thou shalt not eat any abominable thing." All parts or products of creatures containing blood, fat, those strangled, those torn by beasts, and those that die natural deaths, be it of age or disease, are abomination and not to be eaten. We have now taken vegetarian animals such as cows and fed them with flesh and turned them into carnivorous animals, no longer the proper cud chewing animals, and we eat these modified animals—these too are abominations.

Diet Reform is Not an Option

When you follow the principles in the Bible, our bodies being a holy temple, then the diseased, blooded, fatted meats are abomination not to be placed into the body temple. The apostle Paul tells us in 1 Corinthians 6:19, "What? know ye not that your body is the temple of the Holy Ghost which is in you, which ye have of God, and ye are not your own?" Knowledge has increased, and we can tell without doubt whether certain clean animals have become abominations. In Daniel 12:4 we read, "But thou, O Daniel, shut up the words, and seal the book, even to the time of the end: many shall run to and fro, and knowledge shall be increased." Let us examine some of this increased knowledge and assess the condition of animal products for our diet.

In 2001 Farm Sanctuary (http://farmsanctuary.org; http://nodowners.org) produced data obtained from the United States Department of Agriculture (USDA) under the Freedom of Information Act indicating 37 diseases approved by the USDA for use in the human food supply. I will mention only 14 of these diseases. Please ask yourself if these diseased animals and the products of such animals are not abominations prohibited by God for the body temple:

1. Actinomycosis – an infection caused by certain actinomyetes may result in bony degeneration of the jaw, and abscesses in the lungs, intestines, etc.
2. Cysticerosis – cysts in tissues form the lumps that define cysticercosis
3. Cystitis – inflammation of the urinary bladder
4. Edema – an abnormal accumulation of fluid in cells, tissues, or cavities of the body
5. Endocarditis – infection of the heart valves and parts of the inside lining of the heart muscle, known as the endocardium
6. Enteritis – inflammation of the intestine, especially small intestine

7. Epithelioma – tumor composed mostly of epithelial cells, which is a malignant skin tumor
8. Gangrene – the decay of tissue in a part of the body when the blood supply is obstructed
9. Hepatitis – inflammation of the liver, often accompanied by jaundice and fever
10. Neoplasms – an abnormal growth of tissue, as a tumor
11. Nephritis – acute or chronic disease of the kidneys, characterized by inflammation, degeneration, and fibrosis
12. Neurofibroma – a tumor that consists of nerve fibers and connective tissues, caused by an abnormal proliferation of Schwann cells
13. Pneumonia – inflammation or infection of the alveoli of the lungs of varying degrees and severity, caused by bacteria, virus, etc.
14. Pyometra – an abscessed, pus-filled infected uterus. Toxins and bacteria leak across the uterine walls and into the bloodstream causing life-threatening toxic effects. Without treatment death is inevitable.

Saints, judge for yourself if these diseased animals have not turned abominable not to be ever placed in our body temples. Keep in mind, in 1890 Ellen White, a prophet of God, wrote, "Again and again I have been shown that God is trying to lead us back, step by step, to His original design—that man should subsist upon the natural products of the earth" (*Counsels on Health*, p. 450).

In 1905 Ellen White wrote, "Is it not time that all should aim to dispense with flesh foods? How can those who are seeking to become pure, refined, and holy, that they may have the companionship of heavenly angels, continue to use as food anything that has so harmful an effect on soul and body? How can they take the life of God's creatures that they may consume the flesh as a luxury? Let them, rather, return

Diet Reform is Not an Option

to the wholesome and delicious food given to man in the beginning, and themselves practice, and teach their children to practice, mercy toward the dumb creatures that God has made and has placed under our dominion" (*The Ministry of Healing*, p. 317).

In 2005 Dr Campbell and other renowned scientists published a report on what came to be known as *The China Study* (http://thechinastudy.com), which was published as a book in 2006. The study was a 20-year partnership of Cornell University, Oxford University, and the Chinese Academy of Preventive Medicine, taking a survey of diseases and lifestyle factors in rural China and Taiwan. The study was recognized by *The New York Times* as the "most comprehensive large study ever undertaken of the relationship between diet and the risk of developing disease."

The study concluded that "people who ate the most animal-based foods got the most chronic disease . . . People who ate the most plant-based foods were the healthiest and tended to avoid chronic disease." The study results could not be ignored. Of the animal products, milk was found to pose the most danger for cancer. Judge for yourself if the cancerous elements in milk do not turn milk into an abominable thing not to be placed into the body temple.

Following is an excerpt from the book: "As we have seen with other forms of cancer, large-scale observational studies show a link between prostrate cancer and an animal-based diet, particularly one based heavily on diary . . . Animal protein causes the body to produce more IGF-1 [Insulin-like Growth Factor 1], which in turn throws cell growth and removal out of whack, stimulating cancer development. Animal protein suppresses the production of 'supercharged' [vitamin] D. Excessive calcium, as found in [animal] milk, also suppresses the production of 'supercharged' D. 'Supercharged' D is responsible for creating a wide variety of health benefits in the body. Persistently low

Awakening the Remnant

levels of supercharged D create an inviting environment for different cancers, autoimmune diseases, osteoporosis and other diseases . . .

"Of the people you know who have cancer, or are at risk of having cancer, how many of them have considered the possibility of adopting a whole foods, plant-based diet to improve their chances? . . . Food as a key to health represents a powerful challenge to conventional medicine, which is fundamentally built on drugs and surgery. The widespread communities of nutrition professionals, researchers and doctors are, as a whole, either unaware of this evidence or reluctant to share it . . .

"There is enough evidence now that cancer alliances, and prostrate and colon cancer institutions, should be discussing the possibility of providing information everywhere on how a whole foods, plant-based diet may be an incredibly effective anti-cancer medicine" (T. Colin Campbell and Thomas M. Campbell, *The China Study – The Most Comprehensive Study of Nutrition Ever Conducted and the Startling Implications for Diet, Weight Loss and Long-term Health*, pp. 179-182). This is indeed startling evidence!

Startling scientific evidence apart, as remnants, we need to go back to the Israelites and examine them in Babylon. In the book of Daniel, we find that people like Daniel followed the plant-based diet, and in the end they were the only ones who did not worship the statue made by King Nebuchadnezzar.

Daniel said, "Let them give us pulse to eat and water to drink" (Dan. 1:12). Ellen White puts the history into perspective: "As Daniel and his fellows were brought to the test, they placed themselves fully on the side of righteousness and truth. They did not move capriciously, but intelligently. They decided that as flesh-meat had not composed their diet in the past, it should not come into their diet in the future, and as wine had been prohibited to all who should engage in the service of God, they determined that they would not partake of

Diet Reform is Not an Option

it. The fate of the sons of Aaron had been presented before them, and they knew that the use of wine would confuse their senses, that the indulgence of appetite would be-cloud their powers of discernment. These particulars were placed on record in the history of the children of Israel as a warning to every youth to avoid all customs and practises and indulgences that would in any way dishonor God" (*S.D.A. Bible Commentary*, vol. 4, p. 1166).

In contrast to the Israelites in old Babylon, we the remnant are also living in this corrupted world. We see here in these last days that the Lord sends a call to His people. In Revelation 18:2-4 it says, "Babylon the great is fallen . . . the merchants of the earth are waxed rich through the abundance of her delicacies. . . . Come out of her, my people, that ye be not partakers of her sins, and that ye receive not of her plagues." Whenever you read prophecy and symbolic terms such as "Babylon" are used, study the types and parallel in the Bible. We read about God's people in Babylon of old.

In Daniel 1:11-14 we see that Daniel and his three Hebrew friends had long read the history of God's children in the wilderness where God sought to remove a flesh diet and return them to the original diet. They knew the conditions of meats in Babylon were not fit for God's people, and they refused to eat meats served in Babylon. We too must make the same intelligent decision about flesh meats in the world or we may be lost.

Do we, as a remnant of God, need the world to educate us on diet reform? No! As Seventh-day Adventists these scientific revelations do not tell us anything new. For well over a hundred years we have enjoyed the tremendous advantage of holding the truth about health and of having special divine counsel on the subject of nutrition and diet. Unfortunately for us, we have, in the majority, only paid lip service to diet and general health reform.

Awakening the Remnant

Our strongest and most unique contributions to health issues have been through the Spirit of Prophecy, in the writings of Ellen White in the area of diet and disease. Over a period of years, in which almost nothing was being said on the subject of nutrition, Ellen White gave God's message repeatedly that meat eating was a basic cause of disease, including cancer. Ellen White wrote, "People are continually eating flesh that is filled with tuberculosis and cancerous germs. Tuberculosis, cancer, and other fatal diseases are thus communicated" (*The Ministry of Healing*, p. 313). In 1909 Ellen White emphatically wrote, "If meat eating was ever healthful, it is not safe now. Cancers, tumors, and pulmonary diseases are largely caused by meat eating" (*Counsels on Health*, p. 133).

The scientific world has since caught up with divine revelation that we as Seventh-day Adventists have held for years. We have largely not been moved by the divine counsel. But what can be said to impress Seventh-day Adventists who have not been impressed by the clear statements of inspiration? Those who are ruled by appetite rather than principle will be no more moved by scientific fact than by divine counsel. In the light of indisputable evidence, some still feed on hot dogs that contain a mishmash of animal ears, feet, snouts, udders, brains, bladders, eyes, tongues, and blood. What an abomination to put in the body temple!

What can be said to persuade fellow Seventh-day Adventists to not eat meats? Let us remind ourselves of the principles we looked at earlier. Blood in animals must not be eaten (Lev. 3:17; Acts 15:29). If for argument sake we forget about the diseases in animals, what are we going to do about the New Testament law concerning the eating of blood? The inspired leaders of the early church spent long hours discussing the basic requirements for Gentile membership in the church. Their conclusion is recorded in Acts 15:19 and 20, where James speaks for the entire General Conference of his time: "Wherefore my

Diet Reform is Not an Option

sentence is, that we trouble not them, which from among the Gentiles are turned to God: But that we write unto them, that they abstain from pollutions of idols, and from fornication, and from things strangled, and from blood." Yes, you read it well, abstain from things strangled, and from blood.

Saints, how can anyone abstain from eating blood when he feeds on the marketplace variety of slaughtered animals? The flesh is gorged with blood sometimes artificially injected to give a healthy color to rotting meat. To follow the prescribed biblical laws of draining all blood from the animal would render the flesh almost tasteless. Few are willing to deny their craving for animal blood in order to meet the requirements of the Word of God. Various semantically manipulated interpretations have been devised to justify eating the blood, but most carnivorous Seventh-day Adventists uncomfortably skim past Acts 15. They assume that the New Testament law must refer to drinking blood, instead of eating it in the animal. But that is not the basis for proscribing blood in the Old Testament (Lev. 3:17). Why should it be different in the New Testament (Acts 15:20, 29)? It is surely something for Seventh-day Adventists to weigh carefully, especially in the light of additional counsel. Serious remnants should be well awake by now.

Knowing what we know today about animal products (the Farm-Sanctuary data, *The China Study* findings), should we indulge in foods that have turned abominable and place them in the body temple and teach others to do so? Should God's chosen people be the source of defilement of body temples or should we share the pure health reform message? If God sends messengers to cry out loud against defiling the body temple and making of no effect the health reform message, should we lift up our hands against God's messengers? If we continue to ignore the warnings in the Bible, the Spirit of Prophecy reproofs, the increased scientific knowledge in the world, and shun a plant-

Awakening the Remnant

based diet, there remains no remedy. These words will be said of us: "But they mocked the messengers of God, and despised his words, and misused his prophets, until the wrath of the LORD arose against his people, till there was no remedy" (2 Chron. 36:16).

You may ask, is the Spirit of Prophecy silent on the effect of flesh eating? The answer is no; God has given us more than enough warnings about the dangers of flesh. Following are a few statements from Ellen White. But first we remind ourselves of the master plan of Satan to ensnare us using appetite: "They may think themselves safe because they believe the truth, but indulgence of appetite or the lower passions, which will confuse judgment and destroy discrimination, will cause their fall" (*Testimonies to Ministers and Gospel Workers*, p. 473).

Now let us read a few more quotes: "As a people we have been given the work of making known the principles of health reform. There are some who think that the question of diet is not of sufficient importance to be included in their evangelistic work. But such make a great mistake. God's word declares, 'Whether therefore ye eat, or drink, or whatsoever ye do, do all to the glory of God.' 1 Corinthians 10:31. The subject of temperance, in all its bearings, has an important place in the work of salvation" (*Testimonies for the Church*, vol. 9, p. 112).

"Again I will refer to the diet question. We cannot now do as we have ventured to do in the past in regard to meat eating. It has always been a curse to the human family, but now it is made particularly so in the curse which God has pronounced upon the herds of the field, because of man's transgression and sin. The disease upon animals is becoming more and more common, and our only safety now is in leaving meat entirely alone" (*Counsels on Diet and Foods*, p. 412).

Ellen White also wrote, "Is it not time that all should aim to dispense with flesh foods? How can those who are seeking to become pure, refined, and holy, that they may have the companionship of heavenly angels, continue to use as food anything that has so harmful an

Diet Reform is Not an Option

effect on soul and body? How can they take the life of God's creatures that they may consume the flesh as a luxury? Let them, rather, return to the wholesome and delicious food given to man in the beginning, and themselves practice, and teach their children to practice, mercy toward the dumb creatures that God has made and has placed under our dominion" (*Counsels on Diet and Foods*, p. 380).

"Those who indulge in meat eating, tea drinking, and gluttony are sowing seeds for a harvest of pain and death. The unhealthful food placed in the stomach strengthens the appetites that war against the soul, developing the lower propensities. A diet of flesh meat tends to develop animalism. A development of animalism lessens spirituality, rendering the mind incapable of understanding truth" (*Counsels on Health*, p. 575).

With so much in the Spirit of Prophecy against an animal-based diet, are our ministers doing enough to tell the members? Maybe they do not know or they are also ensnared by appetite. Whatever they are doing, the prophet gives a stun rebuke to our ministers: "Let not any of our ministers set an evil example in the eating of flesh-meat. Let them and their families live up to the light of health reform. Let not our ministers animalize their own nature and the nature of their children. Children whose desires have not been restrained, are tempted not only to indulge in the common habits of intemperance, but to give loose rein to their lower passions, and to disregard purity and virtue. These are led on by Satan not only to corrupt their own bodies, but to whisper their evil communications to others" (*Medical Ministry*, p. 281).

Whereas ministers must be exemplary, we risk perishing if we make them our examples, for "Thus saith the LORD; Cursed be the man that trusteth in man, and maketh flesh his arm, and whose heart departeth from the LORD" (Jer. 17:5).

To our tithe-supported ministers, the prophet was uncompromising in asking the following soul searching questions: "As God's mes-

Awakening the Remnant

sengers, shall we not say to the people, 'Whether therefore ye eat, or drink, or whatsoever ye do, do all to the glory of God'? 1 Corinthians 10:31. Shall we not bear a decided testimony against the indulgence of perverted appetite? Will any who are ministers of the gospel, proclaiming the most solemn truth ever given to mortals, set an example in returning to the fleshpots of Egypt? Will those who are supported by the tithe from God's storehouse permit themselves by self-indulgence to poison the life-giving current flowing through their veins? Will they disregard the light and warnings that God has given them?" (Ellen G. White, *Counsels on Diet and Foods*, p. 404).

It is true that Christ assigns to us the duty to support by tithe both the preaching of the gospel and spreading of printed publications. The prophet wrote, "But while some go forth to preach, He calls upon others to answer to His claims upon them for tithes and offerings with which to support the ministry and to spread the printed truth all over the land" (*Testimonies for the Church*, vol. 4, p. 472).

It is also true that Christ does not expect us to support the work with tithe without regard on how the money is used. The prophet wrote, "The churches must arouse. The members must awake out of sleep and begin to inquire, How is the money which we put into the treasury being used? The Lord desires that a close search be made" (*The Kress Collection*, p. 120).

One of the signs that should lead any serious remnant to inquire is disregard of diet reform by our ministers. If they indulge in appetite, setting an "evil example," the question you must ask is whether such indulgence must be paid for by God's tithe at the peril of God's people that may follow such an evil example.

Ministers—who bear the burden for souls, which a true gospel minister must feel when presenting a message of solemn warning to those in peril, who will perish in their darkness unless they accept the light of truth—must live the present truth. If they continually in-

Diet Reform is Not an Option

dulge their appetite, by such evil example, they lower the standards and imperil souls. To allow such ministers to continue receiving tithe money, the prophet said, " It would be poor policy to support from the treasury of God those who really mar and injure His work, and who are constantly lowering the standard of Christianity" (*Testimonies for the Church*, vol. 3, p. 553). We set such ministers up for a curse by allowing them to remain in ministry, and we set ourselves up for a curse by funding God's sacred money to a system that blinds itself to the lowering of standards.

If the inquiry will not or has not helped, there being clear disregard of diet reform by ministers, serious remnants should not hesitate to ask God for where to return God's money. If in such places ministers who have not repented will dare to feel deprived of the means, the prophet answers back: "Do not worry lest some means shall go direct to those who are trying to do missionary work in a quiet and effective way. All the means is not to be handled by one agency or organization. There is much business to be done conscientiously for the cause of God" (*Spalding and Magan Collection,* p. 421).

In the same letter, where some sisters appropriated their tithe directly to certain ministers and leaders of the time complained, the prophet responded: "In regard to the colored work in the South, that field has been and is still being robbed of the means that should come to the workers of that field. If there have been cases where our sisters have appropriated their tithe to the support of the ministers working for the colored people in the South, let every man, if he is wise, hold his peace" (*Spalding and Magan Collection,* p. 215).

Diet reform is not an option open to ministers in the Seventh-day Adventist Church. Ministers corrupted by appetite should repent or should not be supported by tithe. However, remnants should never appropriate God's money to any place without His approval. At any rate, until the end of this world, when Jesus finally says, "It is finished,"

Awakening the Remnant

tithe and offerings should never be withheld. As long as God's guidance is prayerfully sought, God's means should be returned to ministers or ministries that are truly spreading the undiluted three angels' message, the present truth and gospel of Jesus Christ, wherever such cause is located on earth.

Diet reform is not an option open to any Seventh-day Adventist—leave flesh alone! If you have allowed the Holy Spirit to speak to you about what you have so far studied, you will not entertain in your thoughts the lame excuses that Jesus ate fish and also fed people with fish. Jesus is not returning to deal with stiff-necked people who He has nursed mercifully throughout the various generations. Jesus, who ate fish, has since spoken by His own testimony, "the Spirit of Prophecy" (Rev. 19:10), in the writings of the prophet Ellen White concerning His decision about what should be our diet today. If you are merely an Adventist waiting for Jesus to return and you are still feeding your body temple with "animalism" that wars against the soul, "rendering the mind incapable of understanding truth" and you are unwilling to change to a plant-based diet, you may as well give up your membership in the Seventh-day Adventist Church than continue practicing a mockery of the profession of your faith.

In fact, the prophet tells us that "many who are now only half converted on the question of meat eating will go from God's people, to walk no more with them" (*Counsels on Health*, p. 575). Such half converts who claim to be remnants will not stand the shaking, for they cannot bear the truth. We are told that the shaking "would be caused by the straight testimony called forth by the counsel of the True Witness to the Laodiceans. This will have its effect upon the heart of the receiver, and will lead him to exalt the standard and pour forth the straight truth. Some will not bear this straight testimony. They will rise up against it, and this is what will cause a shaking among God's people" (*Early Writings*, p. 270). Diet reform is not an option! If you

Diet Reform is Not an Option

are half converted about it, fall on your knees for God's mercy, lest you rise up against God's plan to have the remnants return to the Eden diet before the close of probation!

Study the first three books of the Bible, and you will see the original plan God had for His people and the departing from that plan. Then compare this with the last three books of the Bible, and you see a picture of God restoring man to the original plan. That beautiful picture is how God is working to accomplish His plan of salvation. You cannot abuse the body temple with diseased flesh and expect the Holy Spirit to tarry with you longer. The Holy Spirit cannot speak to you the present truth while by your flesh eating you have rendered your "mind incapable of understanding truth." In case you missed it above, God through His prophet said: "The subject of temperance, in all its bearings, has an important place in the work of salvation" (Testimonies, Vol. 9, p. 112). So, if those with perverted appetite tell you flesh eating has got nothing to do with your salvation, they are liars and the truth is not in them—be very afraid of them! "Your safest course is to let meat alone" (*Testimonies for the Church*, vol. 2, p. 63).

Saint, pick up your Bible now and study a purely biblical account of God's plan to restore man to original Eden glory in matters of diet. At creation God gave man fruits, grains, and nuts (Gen. 1:26-30). After the fall of man, God added to man's diet, herbs or vegetables (Gen. 3:18). Then came the Flood in Noah's time, after which God then, for the first time, allowed man to eat flesh (Gen. 9:3-5), restricting man to eat clean animals (Gen. 7:2; Lev. 7:22-27). During the exodus from Egypt to Canaan, God sought to take man back to the original diet: a plant diet. God gave man manna (Ex. 16:4, 31; Num. 11:7, 8). However, the Israelites rejected God's angelic manna diet and demanded flesh, which God reluctantly allowed man to eat again (Num. 11:4-6, 18-20, 33; Ps. 106:12-15).

Awakening the Remnant

Let us now turn to the principles laid out in the Bible from the apostles' time to the remnants' time today. In the New Testament time, God sought to take man back to the original diet, but this time He introduced the principle of the body temple that should guide man in choice of diet (Col. 1:9; 3 John 1:2; 1 Peter 2:5; Rom. 12:1, 2; 1 Cor. 11:29, 30). Since the Adventist movement began way back in the period of 1844, God has sought, for the last time, to reform man's diet (1 Cor. 10:1-14; Isa. 11:11; Luke 22:30; 1 Cor. 3:16, 17; Num. 21:4-9; 2 Chron. 20:20). Jesus is returning to take us to eternity (John 14:1; 1 Thess. 4:16-18). In eternity, there will only be the original diet. As a result, there will be no more death (Isa. 11:9, 65:25; Rev. 22:1, 2).

Those hard to convince on diet reform must be prepared to share the fate of the wicked in the fearful time of the last seven plagues. Because "the liability to take disease is increased tenfold by meat eating" (Ellen G. White, *Counsels on Diet and Foods*, p. 386), those remnants still unconverted and eating meats are simply fortifying their bodies with a deadly potential to explode with incurable diseases as health conditions in the world worsen. Once the sealing and probation has passed, these will be left without a shelter. When the last seven plagues hit the earth, the unsheltered remnants will share the fate of the wicked. The internal potential for diseases in the body will increase many folds with the external potential of contracting the plagues. To such, just like having allowed the heart to wander on immoral things, "evils without will awaken evils within" (Ellen G. White, *The Adventist Home*, p. 403). In other words, the diseases without will awaken the diseases within and the plagues will take their toll.

If only, as a remnant church, we lived a pure health message, how much would we reach out to a dying world? In some countries, people are not receptive to the direct gospel, and some have on their doors signs prohibiting gospel-preaching visitors. If only we would knock on their doors with health reform programs. Peradventure they

Diet Reform is Not an Option

would open their doors to receive it, to make better their bad health. We would teach them our practice of a plant-based diet and its natural remedies to health problems. Their physical health would improve. Their perception of life would improve. Their receptiveness to God and heavenly matters would improve. Whether or not they join the remnant church at the time is to be left to God; ours is to be faithful in having compassion to the dying people created in God's image. Peradventure during the loud cry these very people will accept the call: "Come out of her, my people, that ye be not partakers of her sins, and that ye receive not of her plagues" (Rev. 18:4).

If you have been touched by the message in this book, hesitate not to make the necessary changes by God's grace. Saint, no true remnant in the Seventh-day Adventist Church who is reading this book should presume to scoff at the position taken herein. It is serious enough to disobey the counsel of God, but to mock the divine message and seek to make others disobey must approach open blasphemy.

We have more than enough light on the subject of diet reform. To reject that light is to reject the work of the Holy Spirit who inspired the writings. We crucify Jesus afresh if we continue in contempt of revealed truth. "Of all sinners, those are most guilty who cast contempt upon the means that heaven has provided for man's redemption—who 'crucify to themselves the Son of God afresh, and put Him to an open shame.' Hebrews 6:6" (Ellen G. White, *Patriarchs and Prophets*, p. 580).

Sin is the deliberate violation of known truth, and this makes us as Seventh-day Adventists, with our advanced light, more accountable before God. Pastors, church officers, and members should repent before God for ignoring His revealed will on diet reform. Let us prepare our bodies as a pure temple for the indwelling of the Holy Spirit before the close of probation. God forbid that any of His people will rise up against diet reform in these last days.

Chapter 5

Urged to Worship on Sunday

At the peak of the great controversy that began in heaven, Satan hopes to enforce a false worship and to cause all great and small to worship him (Rev. 13:15, 16). Seventh-Day Adventists, who profess to keep the Sabbath, may deny open Sunday worship for a while, but if we have been mixing error and truth, kept amused, patterning after other churches, having perverted appetites, Satan knows that many in the remnant church will succumb to open Sunday worship in times of crisis to come, if not already. It is unthinkable to most church members that any in our ranks would give up the Sabbath and worship on Sunday. Others see this as a sin no one in our ranks can ever commit. Others may sceptically scorn as heresy of the worst order the possibility that some of our ministers may urge us to worship on Sunday in certain circumstances. If you are sceptical of such possibility, hold your peace until we expound the Scriptures.

Bible students will remember the destruction of Jerusalem with its dual application. We pick up the application to our times in Matthew 24. The disciples asked Jesus "when shall these things be?" Jesus does not give dates, but a caution: "take heed that no man deceive you" Then Jesus turns to the things that will happen.

Awakening the Remnant

We read the first phase of things: "wars and rumours of wars," "nation shall rise against nation," "famines, and pestilences, and earthquakes." Then Jesus turns to the second phase of things: "then shall they deliver you up to be afflicted, and shall kill you: and ye shall be hated of all nations for my name's sake." Then Jesus turns to the unthinkable third phase of things: "and then shall many be offended, and shall betray one another, and shall hate one another." Now we may ask: what has this got to do with the possibility of being urged to worship on Sunday? Saint, put down this book and pray for the Holy Spirit to open your spiritual eyes, then read on.

The first phase is a familiar course of things in the world (verses 6 and 7). There have been wars within and without nations since we can remember. We witness natural disasters such as hurricanes, floods, and earthquakes—these are becoming the norm. We have seen poor nations getting poorer, rich nations getting greedy, and all culminating into world economic crisis. The author of sin, Satan, no doubt, is behind all this. His strategy seems to be that of creating chaos and then seizing power under the pretense of putting things back in order.

With the ups and downs of life in this first phase, it may seem we are here forever. But the perplexities of life often deceive us to think that the Lord has been slow to vindicate His cause and bring this first phase to an end. The remnants need not be deceived, for we know: "The Lord is not slack concerning his promise, as some men count slackness; but is longsuffering to us-ward, not willing that any should perish, but that all should come to repentance" (2 Peter 3:9). God desires that we all come to repentance before probation closes.

Our second phase is a time of strange persecution and tribulation (Matt. 24:9). By this phase the nations that once fought each other have united into confederacies, which "will increase in number and power as we draw nearer to the end of time. These confederacies will create opposing influences to the truth, forming new parties of pro-

Urged to Worship on Sunday

fessed believers who will act out their own delusive theories. . . . Men and women have confederated to oppose the Lord God of heaven, and the church is only half awake to the situation" (*Evangelism*, p. 363).

As the church remains "half awake," these confederacies cause a state and religion unity, as a result of which freedom of religious conscience is violated, and then these confederacies demand a universal Sunday worship as a solution to world peace. The now awakened members of the remnants are not compromising on their faith; they refuse to worship on Sunday, and they are met with religious persecution by those nations that have united and religions that have confederated by putting away their differences. Some still "half awake" Laodiceans are confused by this time.

Our 'third phase is a time when our own brethren among us in the remnant church get offended and betray each other (Matt. 24:10). We turn to Matthew 13 to the parable of the sower. The disciples ask Jesus, "Why speakest thou unto them in parables?" (verse 10). Saints, hear the sting of Jesus' words in verse 15: "For this people's heart is waxed gross . . . and their eyes they have closed; lest at any time they should see with their eyes and hear with their ears, and should understand with their heart, and should be converted, and I should heal them."

Then Jesus turns to the disciples in verse 16 and says, "But blessed are your eyes, for they see: and your ears, for they hear." Then in verses 20 and 21 Jesus identifies the people in our third phase who were once in our ranks before getting offended, betraying, and hating the remnants they once loved as brethren: "But he that received the seed into stony places . . . Yet hath he not root in himself, but dureth for a while: for when tribulation or persecution ariseth because of the word, by and by he is offended."

Not surprising, for history repeats itself: Joseph was betrayed by his own brothers (Gen. 37:28), Jesus was betrayed by Judas, one of

Awakening the Remnant

His own disciples (Matt. 26:47-50), and Ellen White tells us that "we have far more to fear from within than from without" (*Selected Messages*, bk. 1, p. 122). The rest of this chapter deals invariably with this third phase of those among us who will be offended.

In these last days, Satan is in the business of planting tares and infiltrating our ranks. The Bible tells us: "And no marvel; for Satan himself is transformed into an angel of light. Therefore it is no great thing if his ministers also be transformed as ministers of righteousness; whose end shall be according to their works" (2 Cor. 11:14, 15). While the remnant have been asleep, the devil has been busy bringing into our ranks his own. Jesus tells us: "But while men slept, his enemy came and sowed tares among the wheat, and went his way" (Matt. 13:25). The Spirit of Prophecy tells us: "While the Lord brings into the church those who are truly converted, Satan at the same time brings persons who are not converted into its fellowship. While Christ is sowing the good seed, Satan is sowing the tares" (*The Faith I Live By*, p. 305). Saint, this is serious! Some of us have no idea how long we have been asleep, allowing Satan to plant tares into our church; we must awake!

As Satan brings tares in our church, they are baptized but remain tares, for they were not brought in by God, very soon these tares go to our seminaries to learn theology, some of their professors are theologians of other churches, and then these tares return as ministers with full credentials. "And no marvel" that Satan brings in tares even as ministers. As we await Jesus' return, we must fully fix our eyes on Jesus, not on fellow members, not on our ministers, not on ourselves, but on Jesus.

The Word is clear: "Thus saith the LORD; Cursed be the man that trusteth in man, and maketh flesh his arm, and whose heart departeth from the LORD" (Jer. 17:5). Given the apostasy these tare-ministers are likely to cause in our church, you wonder why God would allow

Urged to Worship on Sunday

Satan to plant them in our church while we remained asleep. The Spirit of Prophecy tells us: "God has permitted apostasies to take place in order to show how little dependence can be placed in man" (*Notebook Leaflets from the Elmshaven Library*, vol. 1, p. 59).

We are told in the Spirit of Prophecy: "As the storm approaches, a large class who have professed faith in the third angel's message, but have not been sanctified through obedience to the truth, abandon their position and join the ranks of the opposition. By uniting with the world and partaking of its spirit, they have come to view matters in nearly the same light; and when the test is brought, they are prepared to choose the easy, popular side. Men of talent and pleasing address, who once rejoiced in the truth, employ their powers to deceive and mislead souls. They become the most bitter enemies of their former brethren. When Sabbath-keepers are brought before the courts to answer for their faith, these apostates are the most efficient agents of Satan to misrepresent and accuse them, and by false reports and insinuations to stir up the rulers against them" (*The Great Controversy*, p. 608).

As the storms of Sunday law approach, "men of talent and pleasing address, who once rejoiced in the truth, employ their powers to deceive and mislead souls"—even great men who have led our church in the past. We have heard men attempt to preach a health reform message, yet sit to feast on animal carcasses and set an evil example to the souls ensnared by appetite. Such men "have not been sanctified through obedience to the truth." It should be no wonder if such men will "employ their powers" on our pulpits to urge the remnants to worship on Sunday. Never underestimate how far such men would go, as "most bitter enemies of their former brethren," "to deceive and mislead souls." We must wake up saints! Prayerfully study the Word of God—the Bible and Spirit of Prophecy—then stand firm in the truth, and trust not in any man but only in Jesus Christ.

Awakening the Remnant

When Sabbath-keepers are brought before the courts to answer for their faith, some former Sabbath-keepers will join the persecutors to testify against Sabbath-keepers. To make their evidence against Sabbath-keepers plausible to the courts, these betraying brethren will claim to also be Sabbath-keepers. They will lift up credentials to prove their membership in the Seventh-day Adventist Church. Because these brethren have long rejected the Bible truth and the Spirit of Prophecy, they will lift up the *Church Manual* or any other corrupted church policy to falsely accuse the faithful remnants. The grounds for this is gradually being prepared: the *Church Manual* is gradually becoming the creed instead of the Scriptures, and on matters of truth, some of our ministers are gradually referring to the "church position" instead of "thus saith the Lord." The courts will be led to believe that the small company of faithful members of the remnants are fanatics or fundamentals or extremists deserving of death in order for the rest of the world to have peace.

But how can all this come about? You have to look at the grand plan the devil has laid down. For centuries Satan has planted the idea in people's minds that as the millennium begins Jesus will come to earth and establish His kingdom on this planet for a thousand years of peace. Such teaching has no biblical support. Now what do you suppose Satan is attempting to achieve in such a false teaching? The answer is simple: What he did not achieve in heaven he hopes to achieve here on earth. So in order to accomplish this goal, he plans to personate Jesus in a false Second Coming. "As the crowning act in the great drama of deception, Satan himself will personate Christ" (*The Great Controversy*, p. 624).

Those who resist truth, even in the remnant church, will all be deceived. "But there is a limit beyond which Satan cannot go, and here he calls deception to his aid and counterfeits the work which he has not power actually to perform. In the last days he will appear in such a

Urged to Worship on Sunday

manner as to make men believe him to be Christ come the second time into the world. He will indeed transform himself into an angel of light. But while he will bear the appearance of Christ in every particular, so far as mere appearance goes, it will deceive none but those who, like Pharaoh, are seeking to resist the truth" (*Testimonies for the Church*, vol. 5, p. 698). And the Bible reminds us, "And no marvel; for Satan himself is transformed into an angel of light" (2 Cor. 11:14).

We may ask the question: What does Satan expect to achieve in personally counterfeiting the coming of Jesus Christ? The Spirit of Prophecy answers: "That gigantic system of false religion is a masterpiece of Satan's power,—a monument of his efforts to seat himself upon the throne to rule the earth according to his will" (*The Great Controversy*, p. 50). Ellen White continues: "The time is at hand when Satan will work miracles to confirm minds in the belief that he is God" (*S.D.A. Bible Commentary*, vol. 7, p. 975). And what will be the result, you may ask? "Men will be deceived and will exalt him to the place of God and deify him" (*Testimonies to Ministers and Gospel Workers*, p. 62).

This helps us to understand the fulfillment of the last end-time prophecies, for the confederating agencies are to develop a religious world empire that will usher in this long-expected supposed millennium of peace. The Spirit of Prophecy confirms this: "Papists, Protestants, and worldlings will alike accept the form of godliness without the power, and they will see in this union a grand movement for the conversion of the world and the ushering in of the long-expected millennium" (*The Great Controversy*, p. 588). This prediction about this millennium will be fulfilled before our very eyes in our day. "The spirits of devils will go forth to the kings of the earth and to the whole world, to fasten them in deception, and urge them to unite with Satan in his last struggle against the government of heaven" (Ibid., p. 624).

Awakening the Remnant

As the remnant church, we must be very sure that we do not even give the appearance that we are part of the religious unions being formed to fulfil the prophecies that will make void the commandments of God. While we preach the message in Revelation 14:9-12 and 18:1-8, as the remnants, we must heed the prophetic warning: "Danger in Worldly Alliances.—[Revelation 18:1-8 quoted.] This terrible picture, drawn by John to show how completely the powers of earth will give themselves over to evil, should show those who have received the truth how dangerous it is to link up with secret societies or to join themselves in any way with those who do not keep God's commandments" (*S.D.A. Bible Commentary*, vol. 7, p. 985). Whether societies or confederacies or unions or ecumenical movements, and whether we join as observers or members, we must heed the prophetic warning. If we do not heed the warning, we will be deceived or urged to worship on Sunday.

The prophet asks a soul-searching question, especially to our church leaders today: "The Lord has singled us out and made us subjects of His marvelous mercy. Shall we be charmed with the pratings of the apostate? Shall we choose to take our stand with Satan and his host? Shall we join with the transgressors of God's law? Rather let it be our prayer: 'Lord, put enmity between me and the serpent.' If we are not at enmity with his works of darkness, his powerful folds encircle us, and his sting is ready at any moment to be driven to our hearts. We should count him a deadly foe. We should oppose him in the name of Christ. Our work is still onward. We must battle for every inch of ground. Let all who name the name of Christ clothe themselves with the armor of righteousness" (*Testimonies for the Church*, vol. 4, p. 595).

The following inspired statement tells us what is to happen: "Fallen angels upon earth form confederations with evil men. In this age antichrist will appear as the true Christ, and then the law of God will

Urged to Worship on Sunday

be fully made void in the nations of the world. Rebellion against God's holy law will be fully ripe. But the true leader of all this rebellion is Satan clothed as an angel of light. Men will be deceived and will exalt him to the place of God, and deify him. But Omnipotence will interpose, and to the apostate churches that unite in the exaltation of Satan, the sentence will go forth, 'Therefore shall her plagues come in one day, death, and mourning, and famine; and she shall be utterly burned with fire: for strong is the Lord God who judgeth her'" (*Testimonies to Ministers and Gospel Workers*, p. 62).

Likewise the Bible is very positive that in the end time the world will worship the dragon, and they will also worship the beast. The Bible tells us: "And they worshipped the dragon which gave power unto the beast: and they worshipped the beast" (Rev. 13:4). Thus there is no doubt the main issue in this end-time test will be a matter of worship. At this time every individual in the world will be forced to make the decision: Who is the highest authority in your life? The answer of course should be God the Creator who should be worshiped. "For in six days the LORD made heaven and earth, the sea, and all that in them is, and rested the seventh day: wherefore the LORD blessed the sabbath day, and hallowed it" (Ex. 20:11).

But Satan's ultimate intention concerning those who worship their Creator is clearly revealed in a vision given to Ellen White in which she saw Satan with his demons in a meeting discussing how to deal with those who would not worship Satan by honoring Sunday as a holy day. She heard Satan state: "We will finally have a law to exterminate all who will not submit to our authority" (*Testimonies to Ministers and Gospel Workers*, p. 473).

And listen to the results: "The whole world is to be stirred with enmity against Seventh-day Adventists, because they will not yield homage to the papacy, by honoring Sunday, the institution of this antichristian power. It is the purpose of Satan to cause them to be blotted

Awakening the Remnant

from the earth, in order that his supremacy of the world may not be disputed" (Ibid., p. 37).

When this happens there will be only two groups of people in the new religious world empire when it is fully developed. The first group are Satan's multitude followers, who will receive the mark of the beast. The second group are God's last remnants, who will receive the seal of the living God.

The Spirit of Prophecy explains plainly about the remnants: "The whole world is to be stirred with enmity against Seventh-day Adventists" (Ibid., p. 37). In other words, if Satan eradicates God's people from the earth then Satan will win the great controversy. He thinks then he will live forever and the whole world will worship him as God. This is his purpose, his goal, and his aim. And he expects to achieve this by first personally counterfeiting the Second Coming of Jesus Christ, and second, eradicating God's remnants from the earth.

Revelation 13:15 clearly states that the "image of the beast should both speak, and cause that as many as would not worship the image of the beast should be killed." In this verse are mentioned two words, "speak" and "cause." What do these words mean? "Speak" means legislation; "cause" means enforcement. So this indicates legislation and enforcement of a Sunday observance law. Only the remnants will escape this Sunday worship. But if you have not lived according to the light—all the light given to the remnant—do not count yourself among the remnants unless you repent.

The next two verses say, "And he causeth all"—that is enforcement—"both small and great, rich and poor, free and bond, to receive a mark in their right hand, or in their foreheads: And that no man might buy or sell, save he that had the mark, or the name of the beast, or the number of his name" (Rev. 13:16, 17). The Spirit of Prophecy states: "Protestants little know what they are doing when they propose to accept the aid of Rome in the work of Sunday exaltation. While

Urged to Worship on Sunday

they are bent upon the accomplishment of their purpose, Rome is aiming to re-establish her power, to recover her lost supremacy. . . . She is silently growing into power. Her doctrines are exerting their influence in legislative halls, in the churches, and in the hearts of men. She is piling up her lofty and massive structures in the secret recesses of which her former persecutions will be repeated" (*The Great Controversy*, p. 581).

But saints, we should not be afraid because we have a wonderful promise which means that when the death decree is issued none of God's people will be killed after the close of probation. Daniel 12:1 tells us: "At that time thy people shall be delivered, every one that shall be found written in the book." Zechariah 2:8 tells us: "For thus saith the LORD of hosts; After the glory hath he sent me unto the nations which spoiled you: for he that toucheth you toucheth the apple of his eye."

Whenever Satan has directly touched the fourth commandment, the Sabbath, God intervenes directly! Satan caused Pharaoh to work the Israelites "daily" (Ex. 5) including on Sabbath, so God sent plagues (Ex. 7), and then Moses took His people out. When Satan will cause confederacies to enforce Sunday worship (Rev. 13), God will send the plagues again (Rev. 15), and Jesus Himself will come to take us home.

Soon, if not by the time you are reading this book, in keeping with Satan's demands, religious and political confederacies have caused a law to be enacted demanding you to keep Sunday holy. Satan appears, "in his assumed character of Christ, he claims to have changed the Sabbath to Sunday, and commands all to hallow the day which he has blessed" (Ellen G. White, *The Great Controversy*, p. 624).

What will you do if not grounded in Jesus Christ? Soon, if not already, you may find yourself without a job and under a law that you cannot buy or sell. At that time, if not already, every earthly support is removed. You will, if not already, be hated, despised, and held re-

Awakening the Remnant

sponsible for all the troubles in the world because you refuse to obey the counterfeit "Christ" and his Sunday worship demands. Then, you may be taken to court and may be charged with treason. You may then discover that those who you thought were genuine remnants are in the court to testify against you. If that ever happens to you, saint, you are to know that you must stand alone—just as Christ stood by Himself when all His disciples fled and forsook Him. If you have not by then learned to trust only God, saint, it may be too late to learn to trust only God. You must learn to fully depend on God for everything in life now before then!

Now, let us not forget that Sunday worship is more to be feared from within the church than without. Remember, probation closes for the remnant church before it closes for the world. Those who have neglected a call to repentance and left without a shelter will betray and persecute the remnants. In 1 Peter 4:17 it declares: "For the time is come that judgment must begin at the house of God: and if it first begin at us, what shall the end be of them that obey not the gospel of God?"

Saints, as judgment begins with the remnants first, so does it follow after judgment probation would close for the remnants first before it closes for the rest of the world. The loud cry will be made by those remnants already sealed, by then the sealing angel will have passed through the remnant church, and it will be for the rest of the world to chose this day who they worship. That probation closes first for the remnants is the truth you must wake up to now, or be left to perish without a shelter.

The prophet Ezekiel teaches the very same truth. In Ezekiel 9:3-6 we read: "And he called to the man clothed with linen, which had the writer's inkhorn by his side; And the LORD said unto him, Go through the midst of the city, through the midst of Jerusalem, and set a mark upon the foreheads of the men that sigh and that cry for all the

Urged to Worship on Sunday

abominations that be done in the midst thereof. And to the others he said in mine hearing, Go ye after him through the city, and smite: let not your eye spare, neither have ye pity: Slay utterly old and young, both maids, and little children, and women: but come not near any man upon whom is the mark; and begin at my sanctuary. Then they began at the ancient men which were before the house."

The prophet Ezekiel heard the angel say "begin at my sanctuary," and so we have no doubt that judgment begins with the remnants and then moves to the rest of the world. So is probation—when judgment is completed, probation is closed. Saints, do not sleep peacefully until you know, beyond a doubt, that your heart is ready to be sealed by God's angel. When the words herein remind you of Isaiah's words— "Cry aloud, spare not, lift up thy voice like a trumpet, and shew my people their transgression, and the house of Jacob their sins" (Isa. 58:1)—do not think for a moment that the judgment upon the remnants and close of our probation is a far distance thing.

In Ezekiel 8:16 we read of some 25 Jewish clergy who stood in the very temple of God having turned their backs to the law of God. They faced the rising sun in worship to Baal, the sun god: "And he brought me into the inner court of the LORD's house, and, behold, at the door to the temple of the LORD, between the porch and the alter, were about five and twenty men, with their backs toward the temple of the LORD, and their faces toward the east; and they worshiped the sun toward the east." What an abomination to God that His professed ministers worship the sun! If not sanctified, some professed remnant ministers may, like Judas, betray Jesus and worship on Sunday.

Of Judas, Ellen White notes: "Jesus dealt him no sharp rebuke for his covetousness, but with divine patience bore with this erring man, even while giving him evidence that He read his heart as an open book. He presented before him the highest incentives for right doing; and in rejecting the light of Heaven, Judas would be without excuse. Instead

Awakening the Remnant

of walking in the light, Judas chose to retain his defects. Evil desires, revengeful passions, dark and sullen thoughts, were cherished, until Satan had full control of the man. Judas became a representative of the enemy of Christ" (*The Desire of Ages*, p. 295).

Is it heresy to think that there are "Judas-like disciples" in our ranks? Ellen White tells us: "There are two opposing influences continually exerted on the members of the church. One influence is working for the purification of the church, and the other for the corrupting of the people of God" (*The Faith I Live By*, p. 305). Is it heresy to accept the inspired word that some in our ranks are a corrupting influence? In light of the tares that will be offended when persecution resulting from Sunday comes, is it any wonder if the Judas, the corrupting influences, openly urge members to worship on Sunday?

Saints, we are further warned by the prophet: "Then there will be a removing of the landmarks, and an attempt to tear down the pillars of our faith. A more decided effort will be made to exalt the false sabbath, and to cast contempt upon God Himself by supplanting the day He has blessed and sanctified" (*S.D.A. Bible Commentary*, vol. 7, p. 985).

Be not deceived. Satan does not care whether our test comes from within or from without, but that we are deceived and perish. He will employ all means to accomplish his goal. Just reflect on how little the three angels' messages are taught and promoted in our church. The health reform, which is a right arm of the three angels' messages, is a side issue, for some of our talented men still feed on animal carcasses. As a result, truth is not appreciated, and little wonder that some of these men could one day join the ranks of other churches to "exalt the false sabbath" and urge the remnants to worship on Sunday.

Remember, while God has faithful ministers in our church, there are also unfaithful ministers. We need to keep our eyes fixed only on Jesus. The Spirit of Prophecy tells us concerning these unfaithful ministers: "Unsanctified ministers are arraying themselves against God.

Urged to Worship on Sunday

They are praising Christ and the god of this world in the same breath. While professedly they receive Christ, they embrace Barabbas, and by their actions say, 'Not this Man, but Barabbas.' Let all who read these lines, take heed. Satan has made his boast of what he can do. He thinks to dissolve the unity which Christ prayed might exist in His church. He says, 'I will go forth and be a lying spirit to deceive those that I can, to criticize, and condemn, and falsify.' Let the son of deceit and false witness be entertained by a church that has had great light, great evidence, and that church will discard the message the Lord has sent, and receive the most unreasonable assertions and false suppositions and false theories. Satan laughs at their folly, for he knows what truth is" (*Testimonies to Ministers and Gospel Workers*, p. 409). Read the passage again, noting that the "unsanctified ministers" are in Christ's remnant church, His church.

Now read this statement by Ellen White: "The Lord has a controversy with his professed people in these last days. In this controversy men in responsible position will take a course directly opposite to that pursued by Nehemiah. They will not only ignore and despise the Sabbath themselves, but they will try to keep it from others by burying it beneath the rubbish of custom and tradition. In churches and in large gatherings in the open air, ministers will urge upon the people the necessity of keeping the first day of the week. There are calamities on sea and on land: and these calamities will increase, one disaster following close upon another; and the little band of conscientious Sabbath-keepers will be pointed out as the ones who are bringing the wrath of God upon the world by their disregard of Sunday" (*The Review and Herald*, March 18, 1884).

"How readest thou" (Luke 10:26) the above? Are these Seventh-day Adventists or other outside ministers? Let us recount what we know: Satan brings persons who are not converted into our church, these become an influence that is continually working for the corrupt-

Awakening the Remnant

ing of the people of God, we have unsanctified ministers in the church, and as a result, we have far more to fear from within than from without. As the statement begins with God having a controversy with "His professed people," it is very likely that these ministers are also ministers who minister directly to God's professed people.

We know that, "the chief priests, and elders, and all the council, sought false witness against Jesus, to put him to death" (Matt. 26:59). It is very likely that Satan will use the same device against the remnants of Jesus. We also know that, "the chief priests and elders persuaded the multitude that they should ask Barabbas, and destroy Jesus" (Matt. 27:20). Each of us has to choose either Christ (Sabbath worship) or Barabbas (Sunday worship). It is very likely that Satan will again use men in our ranks to persuade us to accept Sunday worship and destroy the Sabbath.

Whatever your interpretation of these ministers in the above statement, one thing is sure: "Thus saith the LORD; Cursed be the man that trusteth in man, and maketh flesh his arm, and whose heart departeth from the LORD" (Jer. 17:5). While we should listen to church ministers, we must know the truth for ourselves or we will be deceived, urged to rise against the truth and then urged to worship on Sunday, by unfaithful ministers within our church. If we are willing to be warned, if we believe there are tare members in the church, if we believe that ministers are also members of the church, we will have no problem believing that there are also tare ministers in the church. Ministers and members are fallible. Our only safety is in putting our full trust in Jesus Christ.

Chapter 6

Victory Over Sin Before Sealing

To sustain the great controversy that began in heaven, Satan has always argued that God's law is impossible to keep. Following the commonly quoted definition of sin (1 John 3:4), Satan knows that he cannot easily lead most Seventh-Day Adventists to sin by directly disregarding the Ten Commandments. His strategy for the remnants is to keep us in a form of godliness while we deny the power thereof (2 Tim. 3:5). To many, we believe that Jesus had victory over sin, but we find it hard to believe that when we abide in that same Jesus we have victory over sin. While we will not worship Satan directly, he knows that as long as we deny the power to overcome sin in our lives, he will still be worshiped indirectly. But we cannot live like that any longer, for all those who will stand the test of Sunday laws must be sealed, and we will not be sealed unless we have had total victory over sin.

The Bible and the Spirit of Prophecy are very clear on the relationship between victory over sin and the sealing. The Bible says, "Bind up the testimony, seal the law among my disciples" (Isa. 8:16). The Spirit of Prophecy puts it this way: "Not one of us will ever receive the seal of God while our characters have one spot or stain upon them. It is left with us to remedy the defects in our characters, to cleanse the soul temple of every defilement" (*Testimonies for the Church*, vol. 5,

p. 214). For the law of God to be sealed in us, sin must have left, for God's character cannot coexist with sin in the body temple. "The living righteous will receive the seal of God prior to the close of probation" (*Maranatha*, p. 211). We cannot be sealed if we still have even "one spot" of sin. Sealing is before the close of probation, and hence we must overcome sin now.

It is in claiming God's promises that we receive the power to overcome sin in our lives. "Whereby are given unto us exceeding great and precious promises: that by these ye might be partakers of the divine nature, having escaped the corruption that is in the world through lust" (2 Peter 1:4). Christian living is built on two pillars that every human desperately needs: forgiveness of sin and power to overcome sin. The Bible defines sin as "the transgression of the law" (1 John 3:4). In other words, sin is disobedience to the law of God.

The conflict with these two pillars of forgiveness of sin and power to overcome sin is the charge that Satan made in heaven against God: that God's law was impossible to obey. It follows from the definition of sin that when you disobey the law you sin. Satan managed to deceive a third of the angels to disobey, to sin, and they were all thrown out of heaven. To accomplish his mission, Satan invented a doctrine of "spiritual imperfection," that God's law is impossible to obey, by implication that we cannot overcome sin.

Since Satan deceived our first parents, God has always desired to restore man to a state where sin does not triumph. This plan is well laid out in the Bible. The first three chapters of the Bible are about creation of man and man losing the right to the tree of life (Gen. 3:24). The last three chapters of the Bible are about restoration of man and man regaining the right to the tree of life (Rev. 22:14). Sin separated man from God: "Your iniquities have separated between you and your God" (Isa. 59:2). Sin leads to death (Eze. 18:20; Rom. 2:6-10).

Victory Over Sin Before Sealing

God calls man back to holiness: "But as he which hath called you is holy, so be ye holy in all manner of conversation; Because it is written, Be ye holy; for I am holy" (1 Peter 1:15, 16). But without supernatural aid, men and women are powerless to resist evil desires and sinfulness. "Without me," Jesus said, "ye can do nothing" (John 15:5). It is to this end that we are to cling to biblical promises to ask for forgiveness of sin and power to overcome sin. All heaven waits for our sincere cry for power to overcome sin.

The Bible clearly teaches that sin can be forgiven. As long as probation is still open, Jesus is in the business of forgiving repentant sinners. "If we confess our sins, he is faithful and just to forgive us our sins, and to cleanse us from all unrighteousness" (1 John 1:9). However, once forgiven, Jesus requires no more sinning. "She said, No man, Lord. And Jesus said unto her, Neither do I condemn thee: go, and sin no more" (John 8:11). Due to failing to understand the secret and source of the power to overcome sin, many have resigned from living a righteous life. Many have sadly bought in to the doctrine of continued imperfection; this doctrine is simply devilish.

If Satan managed to persuade angels, it is little wonder that he succeeds today to deceive many into believing the doctrine of continued imperfection. As a result, many who have accepted Jesus as their personal Savior are confused over the question of forgiveness of past sins and victory over future sins. It is partly due to this confusion that so many remnants are living weak, defeated lives, and will be easily taken by every wind of deception. There is no question that the popular, modern doctrine has been taught to millions that no one can really live without sinning. Many in our ranks are turning more and more to a soft, lenient stance on the subject of law keeping. They believe God's love is incompatible with strict rules and penalties for violation.

Many remnants have read verses such as this: "Whosoever abideth in him sinneth not: whosoever sinneth hath not seen him, neither

Awakening the Remnant

known him" (1 John 3:6), but they live a life given to sin. Ministers struggle the same way, and very few will preach victory over sin. If they try to preach on this subject, many attempt speaking about righteousness by faith, but they twist the theology to leave the audience more confused. As the struggle for both ministers and members continues, the victorious life taught in the Bible and in the Spirit of Prophecy becomes a myth. The sinful nature within now starts to rationalize sin by reasoning that perhaps victory over sin is merely an ideal, or perhaps God knows that victory over sin is impossible hence in His grace He will simply cover all that try their best with righteousness of Christ without strict demands of obedience.

Many ministers have abused the pulpits by shying away from calls to repentance and instead preaching funny smooth sermons. Such ministers, unless they repent, the members need to stay away from! The demands of the great controversy never call us to accomplish the work in sin or in smooth sermons. The prophet wrote, "The Old and New Testament Scriptures show us the only way in which this work should be done. Repent, repent, repent was the message rung out by John the Baptist in the wilderness. Christ's message to the people was 'Except ye repent, ye shall all likewise perish' (Luke 13:5). And the apostles were commanded to preach everywhere that men should repent.

"The Lord desires His servants today to preach the old gospel doctrine, sorrow for sin, repentance, and confession. We want old-fashioned sermons, old-fashioned customs, old-fashioned fathers and mothers in Israel. The sinner must be labored for, perseveringly, earnestly, wisely, until he shall see that he is a transgressor of God's law, and shall exercise repentance toward God, and faith toward the Lord Jesus Christ" (*Selected Messages,* bk. 2, p. 19). True remnant ministers will always preach, by word and deed, "the old gospel doctrine, sorrow for sin, repentance, and confession."

Victory Over Sin Before Sealing

The Word of God gives no one an excuse to feel relaxed about sin. The requirements of God make it utterly impossible for sin or disobedience to be a part of the remnant lifestyle. The new tolerance for sin is not biblical in any sense of the word. Jesus came to save people from sin; He came to destroy sin. Sin will never enter into heaven. "Know ye not that the unrighteous shall not inherit the kingdom of God? Be not deceived: neither fornicators, nor idolaters, nor adulterers, nor effeminate, nor abusers of themselves with mankind, Nor thieves, nor covetous, nor drunkards, nor revilers, nor extortioners, shall inherit the kingdom of God" (1 Cor. 6:9, 10).

Our attitude toward sin must be uncompromising. There can be no question of making sin more acceptable by diminishing the amount of it or changing its form. And the only means of eradicating it is by receiving the fullness of Jesus Christ and His grace into our life. How strange it is that so many church members have now become apologetic for sin, as though it cannot be prevented from triumphing in the life of a remnant. How dare we misrepresent the power of God's grace in the gospel! Jesus has already defeated the devil, and an inferior, defeated enemy should intimidate no remnant. It is serious enough to engage wilfully in an act of sin, but it is infinitely more deadly to defend it as something that cannot be prevented. To say that victory is impossible is to deny the adequacy of the gospel and to negate a large portion of the inspired Scriptures. In addition, it adds support to the original charge of Satan against God and gives a false security to everyone who believes in the doctrine of spiritual imperfection.

Often people are defensive of sin because they have not been able to stop doing it in their own strength. Most in our ranks are quite satisfied that God does not even expect them to fulfill that law completely, either in the flesh or in the spirit. The effect of such a teaching is exactly what one would expect—multitudes of emotionally happy, but disobedient, members of the remnant church who feel that any concern about keeping God's law is nitpicking and legalistic. Satan, as the inventor of the doctrine, is simply supporting his ancient accusation that God was asking too much. He accused God of being unfair by requiring something that was impossible. It does not help our members when many of our ministers have long lost the passion and burden to labor for souls to overcome sin before the close of probation.

Satan knows that sin is the only thing that will keep anyone out of heaven. Since sin is the "transgression of the law" (1 John 3:4), he had to perfect a plan to make people look lightly upon breaking the law and also cause it to appear unobjectionable. To make the idea acceptable to the remnants, Satan actually is able to disguise it as a doctrine and force it upon a compromised remnant church. In a subtle way, many have been affected by the popular belief that too much concern about obedience is a form of salvation by works. Incredibly, some seem to be so fearful of keeping the law too closely that they actually make provision to break it. By doing so they perversely comfort themselves for not being legalistic.

Much of the problem is based upon human failure and weakness of the flesh. Because they found themselves stumbling in their efforts to be perfect, they finally concluded that it was impossible not to sin. From that point it was easy to start interpreting Bible texts to support their weak experience. Satan exploited the psychological bent of the human mind to rationalize, and soon they had developed a comfortable doctrine that accommodated their occasional breach of the law. Consequently, most members in our ranks today are resigned to an alternating experience of victory-defeat, victory-defeat. To them it is the approved lifestyle of a normal member of the remnant church.

But something is fearfully wrong with this position. In the first place, doctrine should never be based on feeling or human experience. It must be rooted in the plain, unequivocal teaching of the Word of God. It is true that Bible texts can be assembled that seem to support

Victory Over Sin Before Sealing

the doctrine of spiritual imperfection. We are assured that all have sinned, that the carnal mind is enmity against God, and that man's righteousness is as filthy rags. But all the verses about failure, sin, and defeat are in reference to the unregenerate experience of a person. There are literally scores of other texts that describe an opposite experience of total victory and sinless living. In every case they are referring to the Spirit-filled life of a converted, committed child of God.

No one who reads the sixth chapter of Romans intelligently can believe that the Christian is free to practice sin. Paul utterly devastates the doctrine that a believer should keep on falling into sin. It is true that provision is made for cleansing in case sin is committed, but God's perfect plan made it possible for man to overcome every sin and to live a life of perfect obedience through Christ. In fact, the promises of the Bible are so clear and specific on this point that it is hard to get confused. And just because one may not have grown into that fullness of faith that brings constant victory, he should not, therefore, deny the power of God to give such deliverance. When Peter began sinking in the Sea of Galilee, it was not because God's plan or power had failed. Peter could have rationalized, like so many modern Christians, and said, "God didn't want me to walk on the water, and besides, it's impossible for anybody to do such a thing anyway." Like our first parents, we still tend to place the ultimate blame on God when we fail to follow His plan of holy living.

Is it possible to keep the law of God? Satan's charge has always been that it is not possible. Listening to the devil, many have since retired to a life of sin. The Spirit of God seemed to anticipate the struggle many would pass through in accepting the biblical assurance of overcoming sin. Consequently, the inspired writers were moved to use almost fanatical language in describing the possibilities for overcoming sin. Instead of saying we may be saved, the Bible says we can be saved "to the uttermost" (Heb. 7:25). Instead of saying we may con-

Awakening the Remnant

quer, it assures that we can be "more than conquerors" (Rom. 8:37). Instead of being told that we can just triumph, we are told that we may always triumph (2 Cor. 2:14). Instead of promising whatever we might ask to help us in our spiritual battles, the Bible says He will give us "exceeding abundantly above all that we ask or think" (Eph. 3:20). And the verse just prior to that one clearly guarantees that we may "be filled with all the fulness of God" (verse 19).

Admittedly, many of these promises are too vast for our human minds to fully comprehend, but surely they are intended to impress us with the magnitude of God's resources in our behalf. If the language sounds exaggerated, it is only because we are too feeble in faith and too weak in the flesh to believe such purity and sanctification could ever be fulfilled in us. We tend to trust our feelings quicker than the Word of God.

The scripture read earlier said: "Whereby are given unto us exceeding great and precious promises: that by these ye might be partakers of the divine nature, having escaped the corruption that is in the world through lust" (2 Peter 1:4). Notice that it is "by these" that we escape the corruption of sin. What are "these"? These are promises of God. The sequence of victory is plainly marked out in this fantastic text. By faith in the promise we become a partaker of the divine nature, and through the power of that new nature in us, we are able to escape the corruption of sin.

In other words, everything depends on the surrender and commitment of one's self to the indwelling Spirit of Christ. "Without me," Jesus said, "ye can do nothing" (John 15:5). Equally important is the inspired comment of Paul: "I can do all things through Christ which strengtheneth me" (Phil. 4:13). That little expression "all things" is the key to victory for every one of us. It includes power over immorality, appetite, pride, and every act of sinfulness.

Victory Over Sin Before Sealing

After He was resurrected, having met and spoken to His disciples, Jesus declared, "All power is given unto me in heaven and in earth" (Matt. 28:18). The disciples beheld the risen Savior. Many of them had seen Him exercise His power in healing the sick and controlling satanic agencies. They believed that He possessed power to set up His kingdom at Jerusalem, power to quell all opposition, power over the elements of nature. He had stilled the angry waters; He had walked upon the white-crested billows; He had raised the dead to life. He had done all these by the power of God the Father without His own power (John 5:30). Now He declared that "all power" was given to Him. His words carried the minds of His hearers above earthly and temporal things to the heavenly and eternal. They were lifted to the highest conception of His glory. Jesus has all power to enable us overcome sin.

The important point here is that when you have the power of Christ in your life, you have everything else you could ever desire. "He that spared not his own Son, but delivered him up for us all, how shall he not with him also freely give us all things?" (Rom. 8:32). There is that term again—"all things." You will find it also in 2 Peter 1:3: "According as his divine power hath given unto us all things that pertain unto life and godliness." When you put those texts together, an incredible picture emerges. By claiming the presence of Christ in your life, you also receive everything that Christ possesses. Paul described it this way: "But of him are ye in Christ Jesus, who of God is made unto us wisdom, and righteousness, and sanctification, and redemption" (1 Cor. 1:30).

Those in our ranks who doubt the possibility of overcoming sin completely should read these verses prayerfully. The words "righteousness," "redemption," and "sanctification" promise us more than deliverance from the guilt of our past sins. The word "redemption" is not limited to redemption from the guilt of sin but from the power of sin also. The word "sanctification" is a word that describes continuous, daily growth in overcoming sin. The word "righteousness" literally means right doing and applies to a dynamic fulfillment of God's will. They are all big words, but they all have the connotation of being set free, both from the guilt and the practice of sin.

Every child of Adam desperately needs two things: forgiveness for the past and power for the future. Redemption includes both of them, and the idea that full deliverance from the guilt of sin is included, but only partial deliverance from the power of sin, is a perversion of the gospel. Jesus did not come to save us from the consequences of sin only, but to save us from the sin itself. Salvation is not a negative thing, not just the absence of something. He did not come just to take away something—our guilt—but to give us something—victory over sin. For God to forgive us and leave us under the power of continued sin would make God an accomplice of sin. He not only counts us righteous through the imputation of His atoning death, but He makes us righteous through the impartation of His victorious life.

As already mentioned, a thoughtful reading of the entire sixth chapter of Romans should produce assurance that victory is ours. We can add the following five verses to its promises. First, 1 Corinthians 15:57: "But thanks be to God, which giveth us the victory through our Lord Jesus Christ." Second, 1 John 5:4: "For whatsoever is born of God overcometh the world: and this is the victory that overcometh the world, even our faith." Third, Philippians 2:5: "Let this mind be in you which was also in Christ Jesus." Fourth, 2 Corinthians 5:21: "For he hath made him to be sin for us, who knew no sin; that we might be made the righteousness of God in him." Fifth, 1 John 3:6: "Whatsoever abideth in him sinneth not: whosoever sinneth hath not seen him, neither known him."

Let us return to the original charge made by Satan, that no one can obey God's law. That brings us to an interesting question: Can a person believe that there is no way to stop sinning, and yet make

Victory Over Sin Before Sealing

plans not to sin? It would seem highly unlikely, if not impossible. Yet the Bible commands us to "make not provision for the flesh, to fulfil the lusts thereof" (Rom. 13:14). We indeed make provision for sin by holding that it is impossible not to sin, that it is impossible to have total victory over sin.

The book of Revelation is addressed to the seven churches of Asia. In each of the churches, certain ones received high commendation and glorious promises of heavenly reward. Without exception the blessing was extended, "He that overcometh shall inherit all things" (Rev. 21:7). Those seven churches symbolize every period of the Christian church from the apostles to the end of time. If victory over sin is not possible, no soul will be saved from those centuries of time. To deny the possibility of total victory over sin is to rob God of the glory of His mission. Christ came, the Bible says, to "destroy the works of the devil" (1 John 3:8). The works of the devil are the works of sin.

If no one claimed Christ's power to overcome sin completely, the devil's accusation would be confirmed. The requirements of the laws of God would be exposed as impossible to obey. Jesus has promised: "To him that overcometh will I grant to sit with me in my throne, even as I also overcame, and am set down with my Father in his throne" (Rev. 3:21). To sit with Jesus, we must first overcome, as Jesus overcame. We overcome by "looking unto Jesus the author and finisher of our faith" (Heb. 12:2). If we do not look unto Jesus, we will not overcome; if we do not overcome, we will never sit with Jesus.

Jesus stated that He had come "to seek and to save that which was lost" (Luke 19:10). Here He indicated that more than just people needed to be restored. "That which was lost" included a sinless character. His mission was to counteract and neutralize the entire program of sin-defilement introduced by Satan. Restoring the image of God in man is a very important part of the everlasting gospel. The work of the gospel must be done before Jesus comes and not as some magical

Awakening the Remnant

afterthought of our returning Lord. Jesus is not returning to deal with sin, but to reward those who overcome sin.

Having read this far, you may still be asking what exactly can man do to keep from sinning? You need to uncover the secret of abiding in Jesus. The secret lies in maintaining the righteous relationship with the Source of salvation. Jesus said, "he that shall endure unto the end, the same shall be saved" (Matt. 24:13). "He that overcometh . . . I will not blot out his name out of the book of life" (Rev. 3:5). The implication is that those who do not endure to the end will be blotted out. It tells us how, in these end times, we must endure. Luckily, Jesus has made a way. We simply abide in Christ, and by His power we obey the law and endure even the Sabbath test and all related time of trouble. To endure to the end, we must fully overcome sin before the close of probation; otherwise we will not be sealed and therefore will not endure.

Willful sin shatters the relationship by which eternal life is obtained. There is an eternal "if" in every consideration of eternal security. Look at the following texts:

"If we walk in the light . . . the blood of Jesus Christ his Son cleanseth us from all sin" (1 John 1:7).

"If that which ye have heard from the beginning shall remain in you, ye also shall continue in the Son, and in the Father" (1 John 2:24).

"If any man draw back, my soul shall have no pleasure in him" (Heb. 10:38).

"If a man abide not in me, he is cast forth as a branch" (John 15:6).

Victory Over Sin Before Sealing

"If a man keep my saying, he shall never see death" (John 8:51).

"If thou continue in his goodness: otherwise thou also shalt be cut off" (Rom. 11:22).

"If ye do these things, ye shall never fall" (2 Peter 1:10).

"For we are made partakers of Christ, if we hold the beginning of our confidence stedfast unto the end" (Heb. 3:14).

"If we suffer, we shall also reign with him: If we deny him, he also will deny us" (2 Tim. 2:12).

"If we sin wilfully . . . there remaineth no more sacrifice for sins" (Heb. 10:26).

"If any man love the world, the love of the Father is not in him" (1 John 2:15).

"Ye are my friends, if ye do whatsoever I command you" (John 15:14).

"If ye live after the flesh, ye shall die" (Rom. 8:13).

The book of Revelation identifies the crowning characteristic of the redeemed as obedience: "Here is the patience of the saints: here are they that keep the commandments of God, and the faith of Jesus" (Rev. 14:12). Revelation 12:17 says, "And the dragon was wroth with the woman, and went to make war with the remnant of her seed, which keep the commandments of God, and have the testimony of

Awakening the Remnant

Jesus Christ." Finally, we read, "Blessed are they that do his commandments, that they may have right to the tree of life, and may enter in through the gates into the city" (Rev. 22:14).

Anyone who believes obedience is unimportant should read again the dramatic story of Adam and Eve. A tiny, physical act of sin led to all the stark tragedy of the past 6,000 years. Those who are restored to that lost paradise will have demonstrated that they can be trusted with eternal life. Through faithful obedience in the face of death, they will have proven Satan's charges to be utterly false. Their steadfast loyalty will be an eternal guarantee of the security of God's restored dominion.

What can we say, then, concerning those who look so lightly upon the good works of obedience? They are subjects of grave deception and are playing into Satan's deadly sin-trap. The most glorious experience of the truly converted is to break the pattern of self-indulgence and sin. Under the rule of the Spirit of God, fleshly habits may be conquered and expelled from the life. Through faith in the promises of God, unbelievable power may be released into the life of one who is willing to give up the enjoyment of sin. The heart of God longs for us to take Him at His word and to claim the power He has promised. Do not try to twist the promises to match the weaknesses and failures of your human experience. The promises mean what they say.

Now consider this and do not fall into the doctrine of imperfection. This ugly doctrine resurfaces in an objection most people would make. Here is an objection that is always brought against those who believe in total victory over sin. It goes something like this: If you believe it is possible to live without sinning, are you able to say that your own life is free from sin? That kind of question is not relevant to the issue. If the Bible establishes a truth, it should be received on the grounds of its inspired authority and not on the basis of the messenger's experience. If victory over all sin is possible through Christ, it is

Victory Over Sin Before Sealing

true whether the messenger has claimed it or not claimed it. The truth is, there is not a habit or sin known to man that cannot be conquered through faith. Remember, victory comes as we abide in Christ (1 John 3:6), and the honor for victory goes to Christ, who lives in us and is the hope of glory (Col. 1:27).

By the grace of Christ's power, we overcome sin from its amplified state beyond the common definition of "transgression of the law" (1 John 3:4). Sin is not just an action; it can also be an attitude. You may not commit adultery physically, but you can commit it in your heart. Anything unrighteous is sin (1 John 5:17). Neglecting to do the right thing is sin (James 4:17)—sin of omission, as in the good Samaritan illustration. Whatever is not of faith is sin (Rom. 14:23).

For example, imagine that you are in a busy superstore, and your own money drops out of your pocket and falls on the floor. You see some money on the floor, and you think it is someone else's, but you pick it up and steal it. Even though it is yours, you have sinned, for you lacked faith it was yours or you will still survive without taking someone else's. Believing not in Jesus' power is sin (John 16:9). Having the thoughts of foolishness is sin (Prov. 24:9). Saints, we can and must overcome sin if we fully surrender to Christ.

Many in the remnant church unfortunately struggle with this simple doctrine that abiding in Jesus enables us to overcome sin. Because they do no surrender fully to Jesus, they struggle with sin. Mentioning living without sin becomes a forbidden subject. It leads them to ask many questions that deserve answers. But in a combination of questions, there are answers. Let us try a few. Can a person be perfect? Do you want a perfectionist friend? Do you want a friend who will see you about to eat too much and warn you of the danger of overeating? If you fall seriously ill, do you want a perfectionist surgeon? How much sin does God want us to give up? If you are married to someone who is unfaithful, would you want him to say, I will try to cut down on

Awakening the Remnant

my unfaithfulness? Or would you rather have him say, I am done with unfaithfulness and I will from now on be faithful? Is God a perfectionist? Does God mind if we offer Him 99 percent service but we reserve 1 percent for Satan?

God is a perfectionist and Satan is not a perfectionist. Of the two, you choose who you want to lead you. When God leads you, He works out the perfect life in you and you become a perfectionist like God. To overcome sin, you must look unto Jesus, and you will be perfect without knowing it. Paul had confidence; he fought a good fight, but he never claimed perfection. Never claim perfection, but never say nobody can stop sinning, never excuse sin. It will kill you, for it killed Jesus for our sake. Jesus told the woman, go sin no more, not go sin less, or cut down on sin. Perfection is demanded of us, because Jesus is perfect, and He works perfection in us if we let Him be Lord of our lives.

Taking hold of Jesus' power to live in perfect obedience helps us cultivate a character that will be sealed before the close of probation. Because many have tried in their own strength to live without sin and failed, they have given up living holy lives. They eat and dress per the dictates of their feelings rather than what the Word of God requires. They are being urged to compromise their God-given principles in order to avoid social conflicts.

Unlike Daniel in Babylon, many are yielding lifelong convictions and equivocating on practices that were never in question before. Couples are putting rings on their beautiful God-given fingers lest people might think they are not faithful to their marriage vows. Families are serving coffee and tea to their guests to please them socially, thinking that God is too gracious to be upset about this practice. Families are producing television sets for Sabbath viewing for their weekend guests. Attendance to movies is commonplace even among our very

Victory Over Sin Before Sealing

ministers of God's remnant church. Occasional drinks of alcohol are commonplace among some elite Seventh-day Adventists.

Anyone still practicing the so-called small sins may ask the question: Will those with small sins be permitted graciously in heaven? There is no such thing as a small sin, for sin is sin. Speaking of the New Jerusalem, John said, "There shall in no wise enter into it any thing that defileth" (Rev. 21:27). Jesus said, "Blessed are the pure in heart: for they shall see God" (Matt. 5:8). Paul wrote, "Know ye not that the unrighteous shall not inherit the kingdom of God? Be not deceived: neither fornicators, nor idolaters, nor adulterers, . . . nor thieves, nor covetous, nor drunkards . . . shall inherit the kingdom of God" (1 Cor. 6:9, 10). John wrote, "He that hath the Son hath life; and he that hath not the Son of God hath not life" (1 John 5:12). These texts leave one with no doubt that sin must fully be overcome before Jesus returns to take us home. Again, faith in Jesus is the victory that overcomes sin. We must exercise faith to claim that great power.

Saints, now is the time to prepare for the sealing if probation has not closed by the time you are reading this book. Cut yourself loose from all worldly things that bind you for false worship. The Spirit of Prophecy says, "What are you doing, brethren, in the great work of preparation? Those who are uniting with the world are receiving the worldly mold and preparing for the mark of the beast. Those who are distrustful of self, who are humbling themselves before God and purifying their souls by obeying the truth these are receiving the heavenly mold and preparing for the seal of God in their foreheads. When the decree goes forth and the stamp is impressed, their character will remain pure and spotless for eternity.

"Now is the time to prepare. The seal of God will never be placed upon the forehead of an impure man or woman. It will never be placed upon the forehead of the ambitious, world-loving man or woman. It will never be placed upon the forehead of men or women of false

Awakening the Remnant

tongues or deceitful hearts. All who receive the seal must be without spot before God—candidates for heaven. Go forward, my brethren and sisters. I can only write briefly upon these points at this time, merely calling your attention to the necessity of preparation. Search the Scriptures for yourselves, that you may understand the fearful solemnity of the present hour" (*Testimonies for the Church*, vol. 5, p. 216).

In preparation for the sealing, if probation is still open, why can we not fight the devil for a few days and finally drive him away? Because the devil is stronger than we are. We could fight him for a month, but he would still be stronger than we are at the end of the month. But we must know that all of heaven's powers are ours through the promises of the Bible, and we receive them by faith. Peter describes the "exceeding great and precious promises" and assures us that "by these ye might be partakers of the divine nature" (2 Peter 1:4). Mighty power is stored within the promise to fulfill itself to all who claim it in faith. Why is it so hard to believe that God will do what He promises! Now let us come down to the very heart of victory and consider the four simple scriptural steps that any believer may take in claiming God's power.

First, ask for God's gift of victory: "But thanks be to God, which giveth us the victory through our Lord Jesus Christ" (1 Cor. 15:57). We do not earn it by our efforts or deserve it because of any supposed goodness. The only thing we need to do is ask for it, and the victory will be given to us freely by Christ. He is the only one who has ever gained the victory over Satan, and if we ever possess the victory, it will have to come as a gift from Him. Let me ask you something: Do you need victory in your life over some binding, miserable habit of sin? Some are slaves to appetite. Others are struggling helplessly against anger, lies, lust, bad language, or worldliness. The Bible says that you may have the victory as a gift through Jesus Christ.

Victory Over Sin Before Sealing

Second, trust that it is God's will to give you the victory: "If ye then, being evil, know how to give good gifts unto your children, how much more shall your Father which is in heaven give good things to them that ask him" (Matt. 7:11). Is it a good thing when you ask for victory over sin? Of course it is! And you do not even have to ask whether it is God's will! He has already told us in the Bible that it is His will to destroy the works of sin and the devil. If we pray for more money or a better job we should always ask according to His will, but the victory over sin is promised to every one who asks in faith—simply ask without adding "if it is your will," for it is His will.

Third, believe that victory is yours: "Likewise reckon ye also yourselves to be dead indeed unto sin, but alive unto God through Jesus Christ our Lord" (Rom. 6:11). The word "reckon" means to believe or to consider it done. Every particle of faith should be focused on that one request for victory, and then it should be accounted as done. Do you remember how Peter walked on the water? He asked Jesus if he could step out of the boat onto the raging sea, and Jesus told Peter to come. But how long did Peter do the impossible by walking on the water? The Bible says, "When he saw the wind boisterous, he was afraid; and beginning to sink, he cried, saying, Lord, save me" (Matt. 14:30). What was Peter afraid of? He was afraid of sinking and drowning. In spite of Christ's assurance that he could safely walk on the water, Peter began to doubt the word of the Master. That is when he began to sink. As long as he believed the promise of Jesus and acted in faith, he was safe. When he doubted, he sank.

Now, what is the impossible thing as far as you are concerned? It is not walking on water like Peter. It is overcoming that sinful habit. And Christ says, "Come to me. I will give you the victory." As long as you believe that you have been delivered, you will have the victory. The very moment you ask for victory it will be placed in your life as a reservoir of power. You won't feel it, but it will be there. Usually,

Awakening the Remnant

the desire to sin remains, but in the moment of temptation, the power to walk past the temptation springs forth from within. Faith accepts the fact of deliverance and constantly claims the victory that is in the secure possession of the believer.

Fourth, make no provision for future sinning: "But put ye on the Lord Jesus Christ, and make not provision for the flesh, to fulfil the lusts thereof" (Rom. 13:14). So strong is the confidence in the appropriated power of God that no consideration is given to falling under the power of that sin again. Victory does not depend on our strength but on God's power. We might fail, but He cannot fail. All plans that might involve any degree of compromise should be abandoned. Someone might raise the objection that this could be discouraging. Suppose the person does fail, as did Peter when he began to sink? No, this is not discouraging at all! Peter's sinking had nothing to do with the failure of divine power. It did not change Christ's will for him to walk on the water. It only pointed out Peter's need of stronger faith to enable him to obey Christ's command.

Our faith could weaken. We might need to be reminded of our total dependence upon His strength. But this does not diminish the beautiful plan of God to impart power and victory through "exceeding great and precious promises" of the Bible. Without faith by the receiver, not even God's promises can be appropriated. The limits are clearly defined in the words of Jesus, "According to your faith be it unto you" (Matt. 9:29). Jesus pardoned the woman and told her, "Go, and sin no more" (John 8:11)—forgiveness of past sins and victory over future sins!

If we feed our human nature, we will surely continue in sin. We feed the human nature when we continue a diet of flesh meat that tends to develop animalism, which in turn "lessens spirituality, rendering the mind incapable of understanding truth" (*Counsels on Health*, p. 575).

Victory Over Sin Before Sealing

We feed the human nature when we read "books on sensational topics, published and circulated as a money-making scheme," of which their "heart-sickening recital of crimes and atrocities has a bewitching power upon many, exciting them to see what they can do to bring themselves into notice, even by the wickedest deeds," then "when the intellect is fed and stimulated by this depraved food, the thoughts become impure and sensual" (*Messages to Young People*, p. 284).

We feed the human nature when we carelessly read all sorts of newspapers in which "the enemy is at the foundation of the publishing of many things that appear in newspapers" with "every sinful thing that can be found is uncovered and laid bare before the world" (*The Adventist Home*, p. 403).

Saints feed the human nature when they love the world, then "Satan makes special efforts to lead them to find happiness in worldly amusements, and to justify themselves by endeavoring to show that these amusements are harmless, innocent, and even important for health. He presents the path of holiness as difficult, while the paths of worldly pleasure are strewn with flowers" (*Messages to Young People*, p. 367). Does this sound like you? Then repent, repent, and repent!

If we feed our spiritual nature, we will surely overcome sin. We feed the spiritual nature by total surrender to the lordship of Jesus our Savior. To do so, Paul says: "And be not conformed to this world: but be ye transformed by the renewing of your mind, that ye may prove what is that good, and acceptable, and perfect, will of God" (Rom. 12:2). When our mind is transformed, we then can discern between error and truth—we purpose in our hearts not to be controlled by appetite and we reform our diet, we worship God in spirit and in truth without patterning after other churches in the Sunday keeping union, we shun amusements and worldly dress that displease God, and by

Awakening the Remnant

faith we claim God's grace-power and promises to overcome sin and abide in Jesus.

To have our mind renewed, the prophet explains what we ought to do daily: "Go in imagination to Gethsemane and behold the anguish which Christ endured for us. See the world's Redeemer wrestling in superhuman agony, the sins of the whole world upon His soul. Hear His prayer, borne upon the sympathizing breeze, 'O my Father, if it be possible, let this cup pass from me: nevertheless not as I will, but as thou wilt' (Matthew 26:39). The hour of darkness has come. Christ has entered the shadow of His cross. Alone He must drink the bitter cup. Of all earth's children whom He has blessed and comforted there is not one to console Him in this dreadful hour. He is betrayed into the hands of a murderous mob. Faint and weary, He is dragged from one tribunal to another.... He who knew not the taint of sin pours out His life as a malefactor upon Calvary. This history should stir every soul to its depths. It was to save us that the Son of God became a man of sorrows and acquainted with grief.... Let a sense of the infinite sacrifice made for our redemption be ever with you, and the ballroom will lose its attractions" (*That I May Know Him*, p. 311). Renew your mind daily, saints!

Victory over sin before the sealing has been presented to you in its simplicity! If you are willing to be delivered, take God's promises by faith! Nothing will help the one who is not willing to give up sinful living and sinful habits. Jesus is not coming back to deal with the issue of sin, but to reward the faithful servants. Before Jesus returns, there will be a separating of goats and sheep, of tares and wheat, of sinful and righteous. By the time Jesus says "it is done" (Rev. 16:17), God's faithful people will have been sealed with a mark of God's seal.

The people to be sealed are those who "keep the commandments of God and have the faith of Jesus" (Revelation 14:12). God cannot be mocked, not one of us will ever receive the seal of God while our

Victory Over Sin Before Sealing

characters have one spot of sin or stain upon them. Those who have not claimed the power of victory over sin will not be sealed. The Bible is clear that those who live sinfully will not inherit the kingdom of God. Among those are "unrighteous, fornicators, idolaters, adulterers, thieves, drunkards, revilers, extortionists" (1 Cor. 6:9, 10). In the city Jesus went to prepare for us, there will be no people who cherish sin. Among those whom John saw failing to enter that city are "sorcerers, whoremongers, and murderers, and idolaters, and whosoever loveth and maketh a lie" (Rev. 22:15).

Clearly, Jesus is not returning to deal with the sin problem. He will stand up and walk out of the Most Holy Place and declare, "It is done!" before He returns. "He that is unjust, let him be unjust still . . . and he that is righteous, let him be righteous still" (Rev. 22:11). Make sure that it is not too late for receiving forgiveness of sin and victory over sin! It is now that we make a total break from sin or it will be too late. Remember this also that before Jesus declares "it is done," the saints will have been sealed. Total victory over sin must be claimed by faith before any human is sealed.

You must stop thinking that God "understands" that humans cannot stop sinning—that is the devil's charge. Jesus overcame and He calls you to take His victorious life by faith! Do not get confused with the doctrine of spiritual imperfection; it is devilish. Unless saints live by faith a life of strict obedience, they will not be sealed for Jesus. If you do not claim Jesus Christ's power, you will not overcome. If you do not overcome, you will not be sealed. If you are not sealed, you will not receive the latter rain. If you do not receive the latter rain, you will not sound the loud cry. If you do not sound the loud cry, you will worship the devil. If you worship the devil, you will receive the last plagues prepared for the wicked, and at Jesus Christ's return, you will be destroyed by the radiance of Jesus Christ's glory!

Awakening the Remnant

Ponder anew these verses: "Seeing then that we have a great high priest, that is passed into the heavens, Jesus the Son of God, let us hold fast our profession. For we have not an high priest which cannot be touched with the feeling of our infirmities; but was in all points tempted like as we are, yet without sin. Let us therefore come boldly unto the throne of grace, that we may obtain mercy, and find grace to help in time of need" (Heb. 4:14-16). Before probation closes, if not already, the message to us is repent, repent, and repent!

Chapter 7

Obedience and Salvation Inseparable

As a strategy of battle in the great controversy that began in heaven over the question of worship, Satan has sought since his defeat on the cross to promote the doctrine of spiritual imperfection. This doctrine claims that grace without obedience is sufficient to save man, that man can live in disobedience yet still be saved. Seventh-day Adventists may deny open devil worship, but Satan knows that as long as we misunderstand the relationship between obedience and salvation, he will still be worshiped indirectly. Satan knows that by such twisted doctrine, probation will close upon many before they are sealed.

In one of the seven churches of Revelation, Pergamos, there was found the doctrine of the Nicolaitanes (Revelation 2:15). The doctrine of the Nicolaitanes is a devilish doctrine that separates salvation from obedience. Like the Pergamos church, the remnant church is in danger of adopting the doctrine of the Nicolaitanes. Of this devilish doctrine, Ellen White wrote: "The doctrine is now largely taught that the Gospel of Christ has made the Law of God of no effect; that by 'believing' we are released from the necessity of being doers of the word. But this is the doctrine of the Nicolaitans, which Christ so unsparingly condemned" (*The Signs of the Times*, January 2, 1912). Keep this in mind as we study further.

Awakening the Remnant

To the remnants, foreseeing our troublesome time, John records: "Here is the patience of the saints: here are they that keep the commandments of God, and the faith of Jesus" (Rev. 14:12). John clearly identifies the characteristics of the saints who will be saved as keeping the commandments of God—aligning obedience with salvation. By the time our probation closes, undoubtedly, we are judged by the commandments that are in the ark which was seen in heaven by John: "And the temple of God was opened in heaven, and there was seen in his temple the ark of his testament: and there were lightnings, and voices, and thunderings, and an earthquake, and great hail" (Rev. 11:19).

John saw the ark of God's testament in the holy of holies, the second apartment of the heavenly sanctuary. The ark in the tabernacle on earth contained the two tables of stone upon which were inscribed the precepts of the law of God. The ark was merely a receptacle for the tables of the law, and the presence of these divine precepts gave it its value and sacredness. When the temple of God was opened in heaven, the ark of His testament was seen. Within the holy of holies, in the sanctuary in heaven, the divine law is sacredly enshrined, which is the law that was spoken by God Himself amid the thunders of Sinai and written with His own finger on the tables of stone.

Those who keep their eyes fixed on Jesus in the holy of holies will see the unchanging character of the divine law. They will see, as never before, the force of the Savior's words: "Till heaven and earth pass, one jot or one tittle shall in no wise pass from the law" (Matt. 5:18). The law of God, being a revelation of His will, a transcript of His character, must endure forever "as a faithful witness in heaven" (Ps. 89:37). Not one command has been annulled; not a jot or tittle has been changed. Says the psalmist: "For ever, O LORD, thy word is settled in heaven" (Ps. 119:89). "All His commandments are sure. They stand fast for ever and ever" (Ps. 111:7, 8).

Obedience and Salvation Inseparable

It is to this unchangeable law that the three angels proclaim the present truth in Revelation 14. The angel announces: "The hour of His judgment is come" pointing to the close of Jesus' work as our heavenly advocate. That men may be prepared to stand in the judgment, the message commands them to "fear God, and give glory to Him . . . and worship Him that made heaven, and earth, and the sea, and the fountains of waters"

The result of an acceptance of these messages is given in the Word: Here are they "which keep the commandments of God, and have the testimony of Jesus Christ" (Rev. 12:17). In order to be prepared for the judgment, it is necessary that men should keep the law of God. That law will be the standard of character in the judgment. The apostle Paul declares in Romans 2 that "as many as have sinned in the law shall be judged by the law" (verse 12) "in the day when God shall judge the secrets of men by Jesus Christ" (verse 16). And he says that "the doers of the law shall be justified" (verse 13). Faith is essential in pleasing God by the keeping of the law of God, for "without faith it is impossible to please him" (Heb. 11:6). And "whatsoever is not of faith is sin" (Rom. 14:23).

It must be understood that as men are called upon to "fear God, and give glory to Him" and to worship Him as the Creator of the heavens and the earth, they must obey His law in order to fulfil the command "fear God, and give glory to Him." Says the wise man: "Fear God, and keep His commandments: for this is the whole duty of man" (Eccl. 12:13). Without obedience to His commandments, worship will not be pleasing to God and ultimately salvation cannot be granted. For John tells us, "this is the love of God, that we keep His commandments" (1 John 5:3). "He that turneth away his ear from hearing the law, even his prayer shall be abomination" (Prov. 28:9).

There is a fearful new theology in our churches, which is not biblical and not supported by the Spirit of Prophecy. This new theology can

Awakening the Remnant

be traced in our official publications, and it goes like this: "The condition of salvation is faith, not obedience," and "if victory and obedience were a condition of salvation, then salvation would be by works" ("Viewpoint: The Condition of Salvation," *The Signs of the Times*, April 5, 2000).

But this new theology is contrary to what the prophet said in the same official publication: "In the gift of His only begotten Son He has ensured to us eternal life upon condition of our faith and obedience" (*The Signs of the Times*, May 6, 1889). The new theology is merely a facet of the doctrine of spiritual imperfection. It is no wonder why victory over sin, living without sinning, is rarely heard preached from our pulpits. The rest of this chapter will address this dangerous new theology.

The new theology presupposes that meeting a condition equals ascribing merit. We all know, of course, that the Bible clearly teaches that salvation is by grace: "For by grace are ye saved through faith; and that not of yourselves: it is the gift of God: Not of works, lest any man should boast" (Eph. 2:8, 9). Therefore it is placed beyond discussion that we can have no meritorious part in the process of salvation. Upon this we may all agree. But what about the presupposition in the new theology that to meet a condition is to acquire merit? Jesus is both our Creator and Savior, He answers for us: "And behold, one came and said unto Him, Good Master, what good thing shall I do, that I may have eternal life? And He said unto him, Why callest thou Me good? there is none good but one, that is, God: but if thou wilt enter into life, keep the commandments" (Matt. 19:16, 17).

Was Jesus telling the rich young ruler to do something meritorious when He told him to keep the commandments? Obviously not, for salvation is "not of works, lest any man should boast." But was Jesus telling this man plainly what the condition of salvation was? If we will enter into eternal life, is it not necessary that we obey God? Is

Obedience and Salvation Inseparable

it not necessary that we keep His commandments? Keeping with this scripture, let us read what the Spirit of Prophecy tells us: "In reply to this question [what good thing shall I do that I may have eternal life?] Jesus told him that obedience to the commandments of God was necessary if he would obtain eternal life . . . All should consider what it means to desire heaven, and yet to turn away because of the conditions laid down" (*The Desire of Ages*, pp. 518, 523).

The language in the Spirit of Prophecy is helpful here as it directly contradicts the new theology assertions. The language freely employs words like "necessary" and "condition" when speaking of salvation, yet nowhere in the Spirit of Prophecy can we find the idea that by fulfilling conditions one achieves merit, a share in their own salvation. A sampling of Spirit of Prophecy remarks regarding this illustrates the language that the prophet comfortably used when discussing this point:

> "As He was walking by the way, a young ruler came running to Him, and kneeling, reverently saluted Him. 'Good Master,' he said, 'what good thing shall I do, that I may have eternal life?'
>
> "The ruler had addressed Christ merely as an honored rabbi, not discerning in Him the Son of God. The Saviour said, 'Why callest thou Me good? There is none good but one, that is, God.' On what ground do you call *Me* good? God is the one good. If you recognize Me as such, you must receive Me as His Son and representative.
>
> "'If thou wilt enter into life,' He added, 'keep the commandments.' The character of God is expressed in His law; and in order for you to be in harmony with God, the principles of His law must be the spring of your every action.

Awakening the Remnant

"Christ does not lessen the claims of the law. In unmistakable language He presents obedience to it as the condition of eternal life—the same condition that was required of Adam before his fall. The Lord expects no less of the soul now than He expected of man in Paradise, perfect obedience, unblemished righteousness. The requirement under the covenant of grace is just as broad as the requirement made in Eden—harmony with God's law, which is holy, just, and good" (*Christ's Object Lessons*, pp. 390, 391).

"Under the new covenant, perfect obedience is the condition of life" (*God's Amazing Grace*, p. 138).

"Could there be an excuse for disobedience, it would prove our heavenly Father unjust, in that He had given us conditions of salvation with which we could not comply" (*Sketches from the Life of Paul*, p. 296).

"God works; but man must co-operate with him in the great plan of salvation. The condition of eternal life is not merely to believe, but to do the words of God" (*The Home Missionary*, October 1, 1897).

"Self-denial is the condition of salvation" (*The Bible Echo*, December 9, 1895).

"Implicit obedience is the condition of salvation" (*The Signs of the Times*, November 15, 1899).

"You cannot enjoy His blessing without any action on your part" (*Manuscript Releases*, vol. 6, p. 18).

Obedience and Salvation Inseparable

"Obedience brings salvation, disobedience, ruin" (*Manuscript Releases*, vol. 7, p. 264).

"The terms of salvation for every son and daughter of Adam are here outlined. It is plainly stated that the condition of gaining eternal life is obedience to the commandments of God" (*The Review and Herald*, October 26, 1897).

"The great gift of salvation is freely offered to us, through Jesus Christ, on condition that we obey the law of God; and individually we are to accept the terms of life with the deepest humiliation and gratitude" (*The Signs of the Times*, December 15, 1887).

"In the gift of His only begotten Son He has ensured to us eternal life upon condition of our faith and obedience" (*The Signs of the Times*, May 6, 1889).

"Entire obedience to the law of God is the condition of salvation" (*The Signs of the Times*, April 14, 1898).

"The atonement of Christ has been made to save all the sons and daughters of Adam from the penalty of the violated law, on condition that they repent of their transgressions, and are converted through the exercise of faith in Christ" (*The Signs of the Times*, August 4, 1898).

"He does not save us by law, neither will He save us in disobedience to law" (*Faith and Works*, p. 95).

Awakening the Remnant

The question we may ask now is does obedience only come after salvation? The new theology example stated above also advocates "obedience is something we do after we are saved, not that we do in order to be saved." It begs the question: why the accent on obedience following instead of obedience accompanying? It is because the presuppositions held in this new theology are at war with the biblical gospel. In the biblical gospel, we recognize that the law and the gospel function together, that the law is not against us but that sin is against us. The law defines what sin is. The law never defines only by letter, but always by letter and spirit. Thus, when we consider obedience, we are inevitably weighing entire obedience, not partial obedience.

New theology in that respect obfuscates the issues with an attempt to project the idea that the unconverted can obey outwardly but not inwardly, and that inward obedience can only be rendered after one is saved. In an elementary understanding, inward obedience can be rendered after one is saved. But it can also be rendered in the very moment of salvation. To truly believe we must also obey. We act on the word of Christ, and He gives us the power to obey. It all goes together. In fact, biblically, it happens in the same event. The Bible states that what really counts is "faith which worketh by love" (Gal. 5:6). That is, real faith is a working faith. And obviously a working faith is a faith that empowers obedience. This obedience is not a carrot dangling just out of reach in the future somewhere beyond us, but it is an obedience that is near at hand.

The new theology employs analogies such as this: Someone who is dirty and wants to take a shower would be stymied if the condition necessary to be fulfilled before getting into the shower would be to be clean. But this analogy does not fit. The condition of obedience can only be met through the power of God. We may choose to act, but our actions require heaven's empowerment in order to come into being. No obedience at any time can be rendered apart from God's power.

Obedience and Salvation Inseparable

We read the following quote from the Spirit of Prophecy: "The power of choice God has given to men; it is theirs to exercise. You cannot change your heart, you cannot of yourself give to God its affections; but you can *choose* to serve Him. You can give Him your will; He will then work in you to will and to do according to His good pleasure. Thus your whole nature will be brought under the control of the Spirit of Christ; your affections will be centered upon Him, your thoughts will be in harmony with Him" (*Steps to Christ*, p. 47).

No amount of washing one's self after conversion through one's own works would have any positive impact upon one's spiritual state. What the new theology in this respect really refuses to do is to permit man to do any choosing at all, because if the new theology were to let us choose, the doctrine must also let us obey. And the new theology cannot allow that because in the essence of this doctrine, this would be to incorporate works into the salvation equation, and works to new theology means merit. Thus, to be consistent with the structure of the gospel of some of the Sunday churches, the new theology must stand where it does. Further, this new theology separates obedience from conversion. This insists that a saved person "must be converted, and conversion, which leads to salvation, is what makes true obedience possible." With no basis for this assertion, the new theology reduces obedience from a necessity to a non-necessity. This in effect lowers the bar considerably and tweaks the whole salvation process.

We need to understand that obedience comes in the same act. We need to see a broader picture: a gospel where faith and obedience function together (in fact, there is no other way they could function), where conditions are non-merit-bearing, where odd analogies are not needed to justify biblically groundless theories and dubious points, and where we find the Bible and the Spirit of Prophecy statements to easily harmonize with each other by taking them as they plainly read.

Awakening the Remnant

The new theology is unbiblical—this is the only designation we could possibly assign to these new theories so in tune with the age and yet out of tune with authentic biblical teaching. Saints, when a person believes in Jesus for salvation, they are choosing to obey. The gospel "is the power of God unto salvation to every one that believeth" (Rom. 1:16).

At the close of his gospel, John states that these things are written "that ye might believe that Jesus is the Christ, the Son of God; and that believing ye might have life through his name" (John 20:31). If we truly believe, we obey in the same act. If we obey, we meet the condition. If we meet the condition, we have life through His name. The Spirit of Prophecy puts it nicely: "In the very act of duty, God speaks and gives His blessing" (*Testimonies for the Church*, vol. 4, p. 145).

This is something that falls into what we could call the "un-difficult" category. It is not hard to understand. It is not after the act of duty that God gives obedience; it is not before the act of duty that God gives obedience; but it is "in the very act of duty" that God speaks and gives His blessing. When we reach out, willing to obey, He reaches back, enabling us to obey. It is a simultaneous occurrence—obedience and salvation in the same act of faith.

Consider the lame man in John 5:1-9. Jesus walked up to him and plainly healed him on the spot. The Spirit of Prophecy puts the simultaneous occurrence of obedience and salvation in this passage: "The sick man might have said, 'Lord, if Thou wilt make me whole, I will obey Thy word.' But, no, he believed Christ's word, believed that he was made whole, and he made the effort at once; he *willed* to walk, and he did walk. He acted on the word of Christ, and God gave the power. He was made whole" (*Steps to Christ*, p. 50).

Obedience does not follow faith; it comes in the same wave as faith. This means an altogether different gospel than the new theology. There is no sliding in this biblical gospel. Consider how this biblical

Obedience and Salvation Inseparable

gospel plugs into the great controversy in a way that no other gospel does: "Through obedience to the commandments of God, our characters are built up in such a way that we may safely be entrusted with the gift of eternal life. Justice, truth, love, pity, forgiveness must be found in the heart of the Christian, for in His sermon on the mount Jesus said, 'Except your righteousness shall exceed the righteousness of the scribes and Pharisees, ye shall in no case enter into the kingdom of heaven'" (*The Review and Herald*, March 28, 1893).

Our business today is not to downplay the law of God, to hold to an ill-conceived idea that "never makes our position any stronger" (*Faith and Works*, p. 112). The ark of God's covenant is open in heaven (Rev. 11:19). The way into the holiest of all is standing open (Heb. 9:8). We are heaven's currently designated agency for upholding that law. For any Seventh-day Adventist to say that obedience is not a condition in salvation is quite sad and a crime against God.

Now, let us look closer at the matter under discussion. Consider this statement: "Our only ground of hope is in the righteousness of Christ imputed to us, and in that wrought by His Spirit working in and through us" (*Steps to Christ*, p. 63).

Our only "ground of hope" plainly has two necessary elements in it: first, the righteousness of Christ imputed to us, and second, that righteousness wrought by His Spirit working in and through us. It is the first part with which none will complain or disagree. We are all quite sure of that being necessary! But whereas the cry today is so often that there are no conditions, it is actually the case that "there are decided conditions" (*Manuscript Releases*, vol. 13, p. 22) to salvation.

"That [righteousness] wrought by His Spirit working in and through us" is the portion that is unacceptable among some in the Seventh-day Adventist Church today (*Steps to Christ*, p. 63). It means that we are changed here and now. It means that obedience matters. It means that Seventh-day Adventists do not share the gospel of some of the evangelical churches. Saints, it means that we cannot go on redefining the investigative judgment as God simply affirming that we are His. The investigative judgment is a determining of our eternal salvation. It involves a process wherein "names are accepted, names rejected" (*The Great Controversy*, p. 483).

What can we make of the statements in *The Signs of the Times* that "the condition of salvation is faith, not obedience" (April 5, 2000), and its glaring contrast to the inspired words of Ellen White: "In the gift of his only begotten Son he has insured to us eternal life upon condition of our faith and obedience" (May 6, 1889). Therefore, what shall we conclude? Obedience matters in the true gospel. It only gets after-the-fact lip service in the false gospel. We must study the Bible and the Spirit of Prophecy for ourselves if we will survive new theologies designed to keep us in sin yet supposedly covered by grace.

Often, due to such twisted new theologies, the remnants have been deceived to think that grace takes away the need for the law. This is devilish thinking. Law and grace do not work in competition with each other but in perfect cooperation. The law points out sin, and grace saves from sin. The law is the will of God, and grace is the power to do the will of God. We cannot obey the law unless our faith gets hold of the power in the grace of God. Any attempt by man to obey the law without faith is void; God alone can declare what amounts to obedience thereof, and God can only declare an act to be obedience to His law if God Himself was the power source of obedience through our faith. The works and faith must act together. John tells us, "Here is the patience of the saints: here are they that keep the commandments of God, and the faith of Jesus" (Rev. 14:12). What a perfect description of faith and works! It is this inseparable combination of obedience and faith that is the salvation of the saints.

As such, to the unchangeable law, the works of obedience are the real test of our love for Jesus. The work of obedience is inseparable

Obedience and Salvation Inseparable

from faith that makes salvation. "Faith without works is dead" (James 2:20). Jesus said, "Not every one that saith unto me, Lord, Lord, shall enter into the kingdom of heaven; but he that doeth the will of my Father which is in heaven" (Matt. 7:21). Lip service will not save us; Jesus requires obedience that we obtain through Him by faith.

Jesus said, "If ye love me, keep my commandments" (John 14:15). And that is exactly what most people do not want to do. If love makes no demands beyond a smile or wave, then it is welcome; but if the lifestyle must be disturbed, then the majority will reject it. Unfortunately, most people today are not looking for truth. They are looking for a smooth, easy, comfortable religion that will allow them to live the way they please and still receive the assurance of salvation. They are hoping to live disobedient lives and yet go to heaven. There is indeed no true religion that can do that for them.

One of the strongest texts in the Bible on this subject is found in 1 John 2:4: "He that saith, I know him, and keepeth not his commandments, is a liar, and the truth is not in him." Any serious remnant must hate lies, yet to John, any who disobeys while claiming to know God is a liar. John could write this with such assurance because it is one of the most deeply established truths in the Bible. The valid assumption of the Bible writers is very clear and simple: If one is not obeying Christ, he does not love Christ, and if he does not love Christ, he does not have salvation. And if he does not love the Master, then he does not know Him, and if he does not know Him, he has no salvation.

John assured us: "And this is life eternal, that they might know thee the only true God, and Jesus Christ, whom thou hast sent" (John 17:3). Thus, we can see how knowing and loving and obeying are all tied closely together and are absolutely inseparable in the life of God's faithful people. The beloved John summed it up in these words: "For this is the love of God, that we keep his commandments: and his commandments are not grievous" (1 John 5:3).

Awakening the Remnant

James says, "For whosoever shall keep the whole law, and yet offend in one point, he is guilty of all. For he that said, Do not commit adultery, said also, Do not kill. Now if thou commit no adultery, yet if thou kill, thou art become a transgressor of the law. So speak ye, and so do, as they that shall be judged by the law of liberty" (James 2:10-12). Those who stand in the judgment will have to meet the acid test of the Ten Commandments. If a practicing thief should seek entrance into the kingdom, he would be rejected. This is why Paul says thieves will not inherit the heavenly city.

Furthermore, the Bible specifically declares that liars, adulterers, idolaters, and covetous men will not be in the kingdom. The Ten Commandments were seen in heaven—the law forbids those things—and that law will judge men. Not one person will be admitted into heaven who is wilfully violating any one of the Ten Commandments, because breaking one is breaking all.

This does not make personal works without the power of Jesus the basis of entering the kingdom. It is really making love the qualifying factor, for it is not until we love that we grab hold of the power of Jesus by faith to obey God. Jesus said that the greatest commandment of all is to love God supremely (Matt. 22:37). He also said, "If ye love me, keep my commandments" (John 14:15).

There are beautiful passages about the relationship between obedience and salvation given to us by the Spirit of Prophecy. One such quote is found in *Steps to Christ*. We read these inspired explanations: "The loveliness of the character of Christ will be seen in His followers. It was His delight to do the will of God. Love to God, zeal for His glory, was the controlling power in our Saviour's life. Love beautified and ennobled all His actions. Love is of God. The unconsecrated heart cannot originate or produce it. It is found only in the heart where Jesus reigns" (p. 59). Saints, when we let Jesus reign in us, it will be our delight to obey God in everything.

Obedience and Salvation Inseparable

To expose the new theology errors, we need to know the two errors common in our church today. We continue to read in the same inspired passage about the two errors: "The first, already dwelt upon, is that of looking to their own works, trusting to anything they can do, to bring themselves into harmony with God. He who is trying to become holy by his own works in keeping the law, is attempting an impossibility. All that man can do without Christ is polluted with selfishness and sin. It is the grace of Christ alone, through faith, that can make us holy.

"The opposite and no less dangerous error is that belief in Christ releases men from keeping the law of God; that since by faith alone we become partakers of the grace of Christ, our works have nothing to do with our redemption" (pp. 59, 60). Saints, both errors are dangerous! Now, let us continue to read how exactly obedience works:

"But notice here that obedience is not a mere outward compliance, but the service of love. The law of God is an expression of His very nature; it is an embodiment of the great principle of love, and hence is the foundation of His government in heaven and earth. If our hearts are renewed in the likeness of God, if the divine love is implanted in the soul, will not the law of God be carried out in the life? When the principle of love is implanted in the heart, when man is renewed after the image of Him that created him, the new-covenant promise is fulfilled, 'I will put My laws into their hearts, and in their minds will I write them.' Hebrews 10:16. And if the law is written in the heart, will it not shape the life?

"Obedience—the service and allegiance of love—is the true sign of discipleship. Thus the Scripture says, 'This is the love of God, that we keep His commandments.' 'He that saith, I know Him, and keepeth not His commandments, is a liar, and the truth is not in him.' 1 John 5:3; 2:4. Instead of releasing man from obedience, it is faith, and faith only, that makes us partakers of the grace of Christ, which enables us to render obedience" (p. 60).

Awakening the Remnant

Now, just in case you think that this is salvation by works—legalism—keep reading from the same inspired passage: "We do not earn salvation by our obedience; for salvation is the free gift of God, to be received by faith. But obedience is the fruit of faith. 'Ye know that He was manifested to take away our sins; and in Him is no sin. Whosoever abideth in Him sinneth not: whosoever sinneth hath not seen Him, neither known Him.' 1 John 3:5, 6. Here is the true test. If we abide in Christ, if the love of God dwells in us, our feelings, our thoughts, our purposes, our actions, will be in harmony with the will of God as expressed in the precepts of His holy law. 'Little children, let no man deceive you: he that doeth righteousness is righteous, even as He is righteous.' 1 John 3:7. Righteousness is defined by the standard of God's holy law, as expressed in the ten precepts given on Sinai" (p. 61).

Before you think we are back again on grace without obedience, keep reading from the same inspired word: "That so-called faith in Christ which professes to release men from the obligation of obedience to God, is not faith, but presumption. 'By grace are ye saved through faith.' But 'faith, if it hath not works, is dead.' Ephesians 2:8; James 2:17. Jesus said of Himself before He came to earth, 'I delight to do Thy will, O My God: yea, Thy law is within My heart.' Psalm 40:8. And just before He ascended again to heaven He declared, 'I have kept My Father's commandments, and abide in His love.' John 15:10. The Scripture says, 'Hereby we do know that we know Him, if we keep His commandments.... He that saith he abideth in Him ought himself also so to walk even as He walked.' 1 John 2:3-6. 'Because Christ also suffered for us, leaving us an example, that ye should follow His steps.' 1 Peter 2:21" (p. 61).

To finish up reading the inspired writing of Ellen White in *Steps to Christ*, lest you forget that obedience is a condition of salvation and inseparable, keep reading: "The condition of eternal life is now

Obedience and Salvation Inseparable

just what it always has been,—just what it was in Paradise before the fall of our first parents,—perfect obedience to the law of God, perfect righteousness. If eternal life were granted on any condition short of this, then the happiness of the whole universe would be imperiled. The way would be open for sin, with all its train of woe and misery, to be immortalized" (p. 62).

Saints, disobedience caused sin. Jesus came to destroy the works of sin, and obedience through Jesus brings us to salvation. Those who believe otherwise, in effect, practice salvation by works. Such cherish their sins and fail to surrender fully their lives to the Lordship of Jesus lest their cherished sins are destroyed by the presence of Jesus in them. To cover up their lack of love for purity, they console themselves with salvation by grace alone. Such see others who abide in Jesus and hence are obedient in all things, as legalists, and find their very presence judgmental.

For years, our members have disregarded our historical standards. Andrews University, way back in 1985, made a survey with these findings: "Our historical positions simply do not correspond to our members' general practice" (*Ministry*, April 1985, p. 6). Since this survey, our members have plunged into sin, sowing seeds of future open rebellion when the Sabbath test is fully developed. Evils that have been practiced through a disregard of a multitude of small things will swell up into tones of sins to perplex the souls in the time of trouble. With the impure character nursed and developed over the years of disobedience, the Holy Spirit will finally be grieved beyond any possibility of return. Evil spirits will then fully occupy the soul. These souls will have no shelter during the time of trouble, and theirs will be to give up faith altogether. They will accept the mark of the beast on their right hand for the want of food and survival.

Those who practice any known sin, to avoid being labelled legalists, are really confessing that they do not love God with all their heart,

Awakening the Remnant

soul, and mind. They will be shut out of heaven. It is the lack of love that shuts them out of heaven, not the act of disobedience that exposes that lack. Only when love is motivating the obedience does it become acceptable to God. Any other work is man's vain attempt to earn salvation and to deny the efficacy of Christ's atoning sacrifice. With love as the factor, obedience and salvation are inseparable. It is Satan's deception to teach salvation outside obedience, salvation by disobedience, which disobedience is essentially a product of lack of love.

We invite you to view the complete
selection of titles we publish at:

www.LNFBooks.com

or write or email us your praises,
reactions, or thoughts about this
or any other book we publish at:

TEACH Services, Inc.
P.O. Box 954
Ringgold, GA 30736

info@TEACHServices.com

www.ingramcontent.com/pod-product-compliance
Lightning Source LLC
Chambersburg PA
CBHW070553160426
43199CB00014B/2492